M000107592

MUSTAFA KEMAL ATATÜRK

LEADERSHIP ■ STRATEGY ■ CONFLICT

EDWARD J. ERICKSON ■ ILLUSTRATED BY ADAM HOOK

First published in 2013 by Osprey Publishing
Midland House, West Way, Botley, Oxford OX2 0PH, UK
44-02 23rd St, Suite 219, Long Island City, NY 11101, USA

E-mail: info@ospreypublishing.com

© 2013 Osprey Publishing Limited

Osprey Publishing is part of the Osprey Group

All rights reserved. Apart from any fair dealing for the purpose of private
study, research, criticism or review, as permitted under the Copyright,
Designs and Patents Act, 1988, no part of this publication may be
reproduced, stored in a retrieval system, or transmitted in any form or by
any means, electronic, electrical, chemical, mechanical, optical,
photocopying, recording or otherwise, without the prior written
permission of the copyright owner. Enquiries should be addressed to the
Publishers.

Print ISBN:978 1 78096 590 1
PDF e-book ISBN: 978 1 4728 0458 7
EPUB e-book ISBN: 978 1 4728 0459 4

Editorial by Ilios Publishing Ltd, Oxford, UK (www.iliospublishing.com)
Cartography: Bounford.com
Design: Myriam Bell
Index by Zoe Ross
Originated by PDQ Digital Media Solutions, Suffolk, UK
Printed in China through Worldprint

13 14 15 16 17 10 9 8 7 6 5 4 3 2 1

A CIP catalogue record for this book is available from the British Library.

Artist's note
Readers may care to note that the original paintings from which the
colour plates in this book were prepared are available for private sale. All
reproduction copyright whatsoever is retained by the Publishers. All
enquiries should be addressed to:

Scorpio Gallery, 158 Mill Road, Hailsham, East Sussex BN27 2SH, UK

scorpiopaintings@btinternet.com

The Publishers regret that they can enter into no correspondence upon
this matter.

[front-cover image credit]

Atatürk and Independence War Museum

The Woodland Trust
Osprey Publishing are supporting the Woodland Trust, the UK's leading
woodland conservation charity, by funding the dedication of trees.

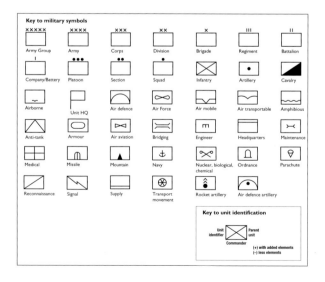

CONTENTS

INTRODUCTION

Any visitor to Turkey will immediately notice the overwhelming physical presence of Mustafa Kemal Atatürk. Portraits of him appear in every public building, official office and most private businesses. (Atatürk and Independence War Museum)

Winston Churchill labelled Mustafa Kemal Atatürk as a 'Man of Destiny' in *The World Crisis* (Volume 2) in 1925 and attributed much of the initial ANZAC and British failure at Gallipoli in 1915 to Kemal's dynamic combat leadership. This was, of course, a retrospective appraisal and actually during World War I, Mustafa Kemal remained a largely unknown personality in both the Ottoman Empire and in Britain. In 1932, the official British historian of the campaign also used this particular phrase, reinforcing Churchill's opinion, and noting additionally that Kemal had 'an outstanding genius for command'. He went on to say that 'seldom in history can the exertions of a single divisional commander have exercised, on three separate occasions, so profound an influence not only on the course of a battle, but perhaps on the fate of a campaign and even the destiny of a nation'. In fact, after Gallipoli Kemal went on to lead armies in Caucasia in 1916–17 and in Palestine in 1918. Later he became a field marshal and led the nationalist army in 1922 to the victories that established Turkey as a nation-state.

Was he one of the 20th century's great commanders? Churchill thought so as have a number of subsequent historians and your current author. That said what criteria might be used to render such a judgment? Clausewitz stressed genius, determination and the possession of *coup d'oeil*, or the ability to take in and understand the situation 'at a glance'. Baron Jomini, whose book *The Art of War* is considered a military classic, thought that moral and physical courage, as well as military knowledge, were also key ingredients in military greatness. Did Kemal meet these tests? Not only did he arguably possess Clausewitz and Jomini's traits, but Kemal had a demonstrated record of success in combat in command and staff positions at every echelon of command from platoon through army group levels (depth of experiences). He also had a demonstrated record of success in all types of warfare and in a wide variety of physically difficult tactical environments (breadth or range of conditions). Moreover, Kemal demonstrated sustained successful performance in combat from 1908 to 1922 (length of combat career). In essence, his was a unique combat record made all the more astonishing by its depth, its breadth and its length. Except for Napoleon Bonaparte, few of the great commanders in military history have comparable records – although Erwin Rommel is a close competitor to Kemal in this regard.

Kemal leading a post-War of Independence victory parade in Smyrna (Izmir) in 1922. There are a number of motifs used in Turkey to portray Kemal in the Republican period. These include, Kemal and his generals, the presence of children and peasants, the Turkish national flag and soldiers. (Atatürk and Independence War Museum)

However, it is also true that Mustafa Kemal was never the 'front runner' in school or in the army. He was never first in his class and second only once. In contrast his contemporary and competitor, Ismail Enver, was first in his War Academy class, married the Sultan's daughter and, as Minister of War, became the de facto leader of the Ottoman Empire in World War I. In truth, Kemal's personal ambitions, prickly demeanour and consistently poor judgment in criticizing his superiors often sidelined his career and saw him placed in positions of marginal importance. This forced him to expend time and energy working his way back into the mainstream. He often faced an uncertain professional future. Yet, his relentless drive and determination kept him coming back from adversity and setbacks to assume positions of increasing responsibility.

Mustafa Kemal Atatürk enjoyed the hard life of an active soldier. He was fearless in close combat and he was highly intelligent. Kemal was relentless in his pursuit of modernity and westernization for his country and ardently patriotic. He lived for his work in a masculine world and he relished smoking, talking, drinking and playing cards far into the night with his close friends. In the end cirrhosis killed him at the age of 57. Kemal married briefly and adopted a number of children later in life.

After leading the nationalist army to victory in the War of Independence (1921–22) Kemal became the president of the new Turkish Republic, serving until his death in office in 1938. In this role he almost single-handedly created a modern secular and western parliamentary Republic, as well as Latinizing the alphabet, banning the Ottoman fez and making all citizens acquire a surname. He chose the surname Atatürk or 'father of the Turks' for himself. Kemal appeared on the cover of the American news magazine *Time* in 1923 as a general and then he made the cover again in 1927 as a statesman. His military and political legacy endures and he is revered in modern Turkey today.

THE EARLY YEARS

Mustafa Kemal (later known as Atatürk and who will be referred to as Kemal in this book) was born in 1881 in Thessaloniki (Salonika) in what is now northern Greece. His precise birth date was not recorded but, as president of Turkey, he chose 19 May for ceremonial purposes. His parents were Ali Rıza, a civil servant who died in 1888, and Zübeyde who lived to see her son's military victories in 1923.

Kemal's mother, Zübeyde. His father, Ali Rıza, served briefly as a lieutenant in the army and transferred to the customs service. Like his mother, Kemal had blue eyes and fair hair. The ethnic origins of the family are uncertain but he always asserted that his ancestors were Turkish nomads, who settled in the Balkans after the conquest. (Mesut Uyar)

The boy had blond hair and blue eyes, which seems to confirm the Albanian origins of his father. Ali Rıza and Zübeyde had conflicting ideas about what kind of education Mustafa would receive, with the mother wanting him to attend a traditional Islamic school and the father wanting a secular-based education. They reached a compromise and Mustafa began in an Islamic school but enrolled in a state civil preparatory school at the age of seven. Two anecdotal stories are told about how he acquired his second name Kemal, which means 'perfection', while in preparatory school. In one version, his class work was so superior in mathematics that it merited distinction, while in the other, there were simply two Mustafa's in a class and the teacher chose to differentiate them by addressing one as Mustafa Kemal. However, his principal biographer maintains that he probably chose the name himself as a tribute to the famous Ottoman poet Namık Kemal.

In 1894, Kemal began the Salonika Military Preparatory School (*Askeri Rüştiyesi*) after which he enrolled in the military high school in what is now Bitola, Macedonia (*Manastır Askeri İdadidi*). In Manastır he formed close life-long friendships with Ömer Naci and Ali Fethi (later Okyar). It was here that Kemal was first exposed seriously to western literature and history. He took an intense interest in the French Revolution and its associated pantheon of Enlightenment thinkers, including Comte, Montesquieu, Rousseau and Voltaire. Napoleon held a particular fascination for him. Mathematics remained his best subject but he worked hardest to gain fluency in French, at which he made little progress. During this time a guerrilla war against the ruling Ottoman government raged in the surrounding hills as Greek, Slav and Bulgarian subjects struggled for independence. It must be mentioned that Ismail Enver, later known as Enver Pasha, was also a student at Manastır but was two years ahead of Kemal. This relationship, which placed Enver forever ahead of Kemal, would continue through the end of World War I.

Kemal finished second in his class and established a reputation for scholastic ability and leadership. This qualified him for entry into the Ottoman military academy (*Harp Okulu*) in Istanbul's Europeanized district of Pera. Kemal did well and was appointed as a cadet sergeant two months after his admission. His dedication in learning French paid off and he was allowed the rare distinction of wearing a ribbon indicating mastery of a foreign language above his sergeant's stripes. Ali Fethi, Kazım (later Özalp), Nuri (later Conker), and Ali Fuat (later Cebesoy) became his fast friends. In the military academy, Kemal focused on military subjects but spent almost as much time studying politics. One historian asserts that he was 'fashioning himself into a politically aware and politically ambitious professional soldier'. Again Kemal excelled academically by finishing eighth in a class of 459 and was commissioned as an infantry lieutenant in February 1902.

While he was a Turk and an Ottoman citizen, the young Kemal was arguably a European in his background and outlook. He grew up in the empire's most European cities – Salonika was the most cosmopolitan city in the empire, Bitola was a provincial town but largely inhabited by Balkan Christians and Pera was distinctively European with bars and nightlife. Kemal went out of his way to master European languages. He studied and became fluent in French and later German and he read voraciously in three languages. He was drawn to western technology and to European ideas in a time and place when such activities were considered subversive and revolutionary. He was inclined towards scholarship but it was during his time in the military academy that he developed a lifelong taste for alcohol, tobacco, card-playing and women. However, none of these activities impeded his academic progress or his success as a military cadet.

Kemal's academic standing qualified him for entry into the prestigious Ottoman War Academy (*Harp Akademisi*) – a staff college that was a mirror image of the Prussian War Academy (*Kriegsakademie*). Like its German counterpart the rigorous three-year curriculum was designed to produce qualified general staff officers who would join the administrative divisions of the elite Ottoman General Staff. Kemal graduated fifth of 43 on 11 January 1905 and was appointed a staff captain in the general staff corps. This promotion immediately separated him from the officers of the line and his file was transferred to a special staff directorate handling the assignments of war academy graduates. In practice, members of the general staff corps were assigned to designated key staff billets and periodically rotated into troop command. Their promotion was accelerated and it was almost impossible for non-war academy graduates to become general officers in the Ottoman army. This was the

'Together with his friends in Beirut in 1906' is the caption of this picture. Kemal is seated first on the left with what appears to be the regimental staff of the Second Army's artillery school. (Mesut Uyar)

point at which Kemal was earmarked by the army as possessing the qualities necessary for high command.

It was at the War Academy that Kemal became politically energized and joined a clandestine group of like-minded officers who opposed the reactionary and repressive regime of Sultan Abdülhamid II. Together with his friends Ali Fuat and Ismail Hakkı, Kemal produced an underground handwritten opposition newspaper. But, shortly after graduation the Sultan's secret police uncovered the plotters and arrested the three officers. They narrowly avoided imprisonment or exile and their careers were saved by the intervention of senior general staff officers. The general staff directorate then assigned both Kemal and Ali to the Ottoman Fifth Army which was then headquartered in Damascus, Syria.

This effectively took them out of harm's way politically, but placed them in marginal assignments on the army's periphery. This was the first of a number of incidents in Kemal's career where he careened off the fast track to high command.

Ottoman Salonika at the beginning of the 19th century. The Ottoman cities in the Balkans, where Kemal grew up, were distinctly European. Salonika, in particular, was a thriving city with the largest Jewish population in Europe. (David Nicolle)

THE MILITARY LIFE

New general staff officers were expected to serve in all three basic army branches (infantry, artillery and cavalry) to familiarize them with the fundamentals of army life and its principal weapons systems. In effect, the first assignment for a new Ottoman lieutenant was something of a deliberate series of experiences designed to give a novice professional experiences rather than an assignment to a particular regiment, which would result in a lifelong affiliation and friendships. Arriving in Syria, Kemal was assigned initially to the 30th Cavalry Regiment, where he participated in training soldiers and led minor counterinsurgency operations against local Arab rebel tribes and gangs. He was then assigned to an independent rifle battalion in Palestine where he conducted training in the Negev Desert and patrolled the Egyptian frontier. He remained politically active and unhappy with the tradition-bound and antique Ottoman government. In the summer or autumn of 1905, Kemal helped found a secret political group named 'Fatherland and Freedom' (*Vatan ve Hürriyet*) and he travelled around the Fifth Army area organizing other secret groups. Believing that Sükrü Pasha, the Third Army artillery inspector in Salonika, was sympathetic to the secret societies, Kemal forged medical leave papers and journeyed to his home town, where he began to organize secret opposition groups. Narrowly escaping capture, he returned to Syria but the group he left behind became a core of the resistance movement. In 1906 he was assigned to an artillery school, and he was promoted to staff captain (*kolağası*) in 1907. Safe for the time being, he applied for a transfer to Salonika and was reposted in October to the Ottoman Third Army headquarters, which was garrisoned there.

Returning to Salonika in mid-September 1907, Kemal found that a mature revolutionary group had evolved in his absence and that he was excluded from its inner leadership. The group was led by Talât Pasha and was a part of the revolutionary Committee of Union and Progress (CUP), or the Young Turks as they were known in the west. Kemal joined the army staff,

Senior Captain Mustafa Kemal in 1907. He is relatively 'unblooded' by combat at this time of his life and seems to reflect the calm of the late Edwardian era. (Mesut Uyar))

which was itself a hotbed of anti-government sentiment, while two other officers who were already stationed in the Third Army area, Staff Major Enver and Adjutant Major Ahmet Cemal, joined Talât in forming the 'internal centre' of the CUP. Kemal, a latecomer to the area, joined the CUP as an ordinary member sometime in February 1908. In June, Kemal was assigned to the Third Army's railway directorate as an inspector on the Skopje line. This took him further out of the political mainstream.

Revolution broke out in the Ottoman Balkan provinces in July 1908 and, when revolt threatened Ottoman Tripolitania, Kemal was sent there in September to quell the populace. He was successful and, though isolated in Tripoli, Kemal gained valuable experience in diplomacy, decision-making and strategic thinking. Meanwhile Sultan Abdulhamid, under pressure from the CUP, re-established a parliament. Kemal returned to Salonika in January 1909 to take an assignment as the chief of staff of the 17th Reserve Infantry Division. On 13 April 1909, reactionary soldiers in Istanbul led a counter-revolution forcing the CUP leadership to flee the capital. Army officers, who were CUP members in the Ottoman Second and Third Armies rapidly organized an attack on the capital to restore the government. A provisional army of two divisions, styled the Operational

Officers of Mahmut Şevket Pasha's Action Army en route to Constantinople in 1909 to restore the government. Kemal is on the right bending over to adjust his documents case. (Mesut Uyar)

or Action Army (*Hareket Ordusu*), under Mahmut Şevket Pasha marched into Istanbul and restored order and the government. CUP member Kemal was the chief of staff of a division under Hüseyin Hüsnü Pasha. Once again Kemal found himself left out of the decision-making circle by Enver, who had rushed back from a posting in Berlin.

Returning to garrison life in Salonika, Kemal served sequentially in the headquarters of the Third Army and in a troop training assignment. Kemal then further isolated himself by publicly advocating that officers quit their memberships

The Action Army staff in 1909. Kemal is standing in the second row tenth from the left. (Mesut Uyar)

Kemal has grown a beard and stands in the centre of a group of Ottoman officers in Libya in 1911. They have volunteered to organize, train and lead Senussi tribesmen, shown standing to the rear, in a guerrilla war against the Italian army. (Mesut Uyar)

in political parties. Nevertheless, he was developing a minor reputation for having a serious interest in military reform and had translated several German training manuals into Ottoman Turkish. He travelled to France to observe the manoeuvres in Picardy in the summer of 1910. In January 1911, Kemal became chief of staff of XV Army Corps and then commander of the 38th Infantry Regiment. He continued to level criticism in public, this time in a written report against army generals regarding poorly planned training manoeuvres. This led to his relief and reassignment in September to the Operations Division of the Ottoman General Staff. Upset that senior officers had failed to protect him, in October 1911 Kemal volunteered for duty in Libya, which was an Ottoman province that had been invaded and occupied by Italy.

Unable to effectively contest Italian command of the seas or reinforce their beleaguered province, the Ottoman General Staff decided to send a handful of officers to assist the local garrison and tribesmen to wage a guerrilla war. The objective was to drain Italian resources and erode their will to continue to occupy the coastal cities and littoral. Disguised as a journalist, Kemal arrived in Egypt and crossed the Libyan frontier in December. He was part of a group of adventurous officer volunteers, which included Enver, Nuri, Ali Fuat and Ömer Nacı, who were charged with rallying the defeated Ottoman regular troops and organizing the Senussi tribesmen to wage a guerrilla war against the Italians. Enver was in overall command and Kemal took charge of the Derna sector in March 1912, where he commanded several hundred Ottoman soldiers, some light artillery and machine guns as well as about 8,000 irregular tribesmen. Kemal organized the tribesmen and led them in unrelenting harassing raids. He became a master of high mobility operations. He also fought a number of guerrilla-style hit-and-run engagements as well as several conventional assaults that integrated regular and irregular forces. His men tied down over 15,000 Italian soldiers and pinned them to the coast. In one of the engagements Kemal suffered a slight wound to his left eye but returned to fight. He was

very successful and attributed this to his ability to impose discipline on his irregular forces.

In early October 1912, while Kemal was engaged in Libya, the Christian Balkan League – composed of Montenegro, Serbia, Greece and Bulgaria – declared war on the Ottoman Empire. This was the tipping point that forced the Ottomans to abandon their irregular campaign in Libya. To the dismay of the officers fighting in Libya the Ottoman government concluded a peace treaty with Italy on 18 October 1912. Kemal returned to Istanbul the following month. His experiences leading tribesmen in desert conditions reinforced his ideas about the inherent strength of irregular warfare and his understandings of how deadly small groups of motivated armed men could be.

Still a senior captain, Kemal, seated on the left, with fellow Ottoman officers in Libya. Kemal and several hundred regular Ottoman soldiers led 8,000 irregulars in the Derna sector from December 1911 to October 1912. He very effectively led highly mobile hit and run raids out of the desert against the Italians on the coast. (Mesut Uyar)

What is known as the First Balkan War was going badly for the Ottomans and almost immediately they lost much territory in Macedonia and Thrace. Kemal arrived just as the victorious Bulgarians isolated Edirne and the Gallipoli peninsula and smashed unsuccessfully against the Ottoman defensive lines at Çatalca, located just 20 miles west of the capital. On 21 November 1912, Kemal was appointed as the chief of operations for the Ottoman forces that had been cut off on the Gallipoli peninsula and was promoted to major (*binbaşı*) a week later. He spent the next several months working on improving the defences against amphibious invasion and hardening the lines across the isthmus of Bulair. An armistice was signed by a faltering Ottoman government, which slowed the war's tempo briefly. However, Enver, who remained in Istanbul, led the famous Raid on the Sublime Porte on 23 January 1913 and toppled the government and installed Mahmut Şevket Pasha as grand vizier. The armistice collapsed and the Ottoman army immediately launched an amphibious assault on the

Dispirited Ottoman soldiers in the Balkan Wars during the cholera epidemic of late 1912. These soldiers have the look of defeat and despair and this image lingered in the collective consciousness of European military planners leading to an underestimation of the Ottoman army in 1914. (David Nicolle)

Bulgarians at Şarkoy on 10 February. Kemal's army was ordered to launch a supporting frontal attack on the heavily defended Bulgarian position at Bulair. Although Kemal's operational and tactical planning was meticulous, Bulgarian infantry in trenches, backed up by machine guns and artillery, slaughtered the Ottomans. Casualties were extremely high with 6,000 killed and 18,000 wounded, nevertheless heavy fighting continued on the peninsula.

The dispirited Ottoman government concluded a second armistice in late April 1913, effectively ending the First Balkan War. However, almost immediately, the victors fell out among themselves over the division of Ottoman Macedonia, and Bulgaria attacked its erstwhile allies on 29 June 1913 at the start of the Second Balkan War. The Ottomans were not participants in this war but took immediate advantage of Bulgaria's weakness to retake the city of Edirne. Kemal's force, now organized as a field army of two army corps, in conjunction with the Çatalca Army surged forward on 22 July pushing forward to the current Bulgarian border.

His experiences as a chief of operations at a corps level and army staff in a conventional war complemented his experiences as a commander of irregulars in the Libyan guerrilla war. In a short period of time Kemal had the opportunity to refine defensive plans, plan and execute deliberate and hasty offensive combat operations, and coordinate a pursuit operation. Moreover, this wide array of operational-level combat operations was conducted in southern European conditions rather than in the deserts he had hitherto been used to.

Kemal returned to Istanbul and stayed at the house of his friend and patron Lieutenant-Colonel Ali Fethi, who was also a CUP insider. Fethi resigned from the army to become secretary-general of the CUP. This started a power struggle in the party which Fethi lost, ending up as the ambassador in Sofia, Bulgaria. Unfortunately for Kemal, his close association with Fethi and his continual criticisms of politics and military matters marginalized him yet again. He was assigned to accompany Fethi as the military attaché and arrived in Sofia on 20 November 1913.

Although he was now effectively removed from the centre of power in Istanbul he recovered quickly by entering the social scene in Sofia.

In January 1914, Enver became the Minister of War, effectively installing the government led by a CUP triumvirate of Enver, Talât and Cemal, which would continue in power until the end of World War I. In Sofia, Kemal was promoted to lieutenant-colonel (*yarbay*) on 1 March 1914. In his official capacity as attaché he passed information to the 2nd Directorate (Intelligence) of the Ottoman General Staff. Kemal was suspicious of the Bulgarians and felt they were scheming to recover Edirne and he also mistrusted the Germans.

The Ottoman VIII Army Corps in camp. Contrary to commonly held notions about the Ottoman army, it was a well-disciplined and well-trained force as this photograph shows. Its principal weakness was its inadequate logistics base, which proved repeatedly to be insufficient to sustain high-intensity combat operations in the 20th century. (David Nicolle)

Naturally, when he wrote these assertions openly in his reports he again came into conflict with the Ottoman General Staff, which was then in the middle of welcoming and integrating General Otto Liman von Sanders' new German military mission into the Ottoman army. Although Kemal admired the German war machine this was the beginning of a profound dislike for the increasing political and military influence of Germany in the affairs of the Ottoman Empire.

The Gallipoli peninsula, 25 April 1915

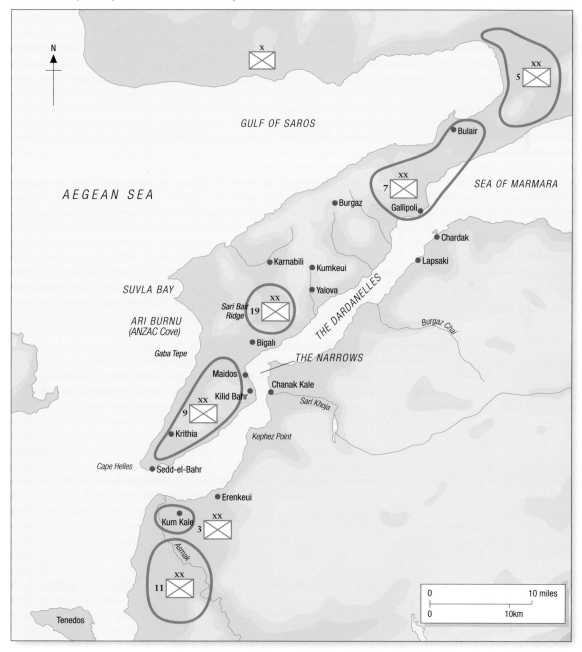

An Ottoman army infantry company occupying an assembly area near the Gallipoli front in 1915. This unit appears fresh and well-disciplined. Once exposed to combat in the trenches, the men's uniforms and equipment rapidly wore out and was seldom replaced. Moreover, there is an absence of protective dugouts against artillery fire reinforcing the idea that the unit is well behind the front preparing to enter the line. (David Nicolle)

World War I broke out in August 1914 but, in spite of an alliance with Germany, the Ottoman Empire remained neutral until early November. As the Ottoman army mobilized for war and deployed to its war stations, Kemal grew increasingly impatient in Sofia. Of course, he wrote a number of letters to his friends questioning whether Germany would win the war and questioning the CUP's war aims. Upon entry into the war, the Ottoman army suffered disastrous defeats at Sarıkamış in the Caucasus Mountains, in the Sinai desert and in the Tigris River Valley in Mesopotamia. Privately, Kemal criticized the army's operations and wrote to the General Staff requesting an operational assignment in any capacity. When none came he considered resigning from the army. Finally, when Enver left the capital to lead the offensive in the Caucasus, Enver's deputy, who was a friend of Kemal's, immediately ordered him to active service. Kemal's new assignment was to raise and train the newly activated 19th Infantry Division for service on the Gallipoli peninsula. Kemal was ready to go and left Sofia on 20 January 1915. He arrived in Tekirdag on the Sea of Marmara in early February, where he found only the solitary 57th Infantry Regiment awaiting his arrival. To his consternation Kemal learned that his other two infantry regiments had been sent to the Egyptian front to reinforce other divisions. On 25 February, he was ordered to bring his men to the town of Eceabat (Maidos) and reconstitute the division. Within days the 72nd and 77th Infantry Regiments joined him, as did several battalions of artillery, cavalry, medical personnel and support troops. Kemal's division now stood at full strength although it had never trained together as a unit.

By this time, events were moving fast in the Mediterranean as the British war council decided to take the Ottoman Empire out of the war in order to

The Australian and New Zealand Army Corps landed just before dawn on 25 April 1915 at what the Ottomans called Ari Burnu. The extremely rugged terrain is apparent and begins almost immediately after the narrow beach. (AWM, PS1484)

open supply lines to beleaguered Russia. On 19 February 1915, an Allied fleet began a series of attacks to suppress the forts along the Dardanelles and sweep the mines in the channel itself. The attacks culminated with a massive attempt to break through the straits on 18 March, by the end of which the defeated Allies had lost three battleships and had three more badly damaged. In turn, the Allies decided to launch a land campaign to seize the Gallipoli peninsula, thus forcing the Ottomans to abandon their defences. This led to the massing of the Mediterranean Expeditionary Force in Egypt which was assigned the mission of conducting an amphibious invasion of the peninsula with the objective of seizing the Kilid Bahr plateau overlooking the rear of the coastal forts.

Poor Allied operational security kept the Ottomans apprised of these plans and a worried Enver resolved to reinforce the peninsula's defences. On 26 March 1915, Enver activated the new Ottoman Fifth Army and placed it under the command of German General Otto Liman von Sanders. The new army had six infantry divisions organized into two army corps, one of which was III Corps containing Kemal's 19th Infantry Division. Liman

General Otto Liman von Sanders. Originally a cavalry officer in the Prussian army, Liman von Sanders was sent to Istanbul in 1913 to command the German military mission charged with the reorganization of the Ottoman army. He did not speak Turkish and had a general contempt for the Ottoman army and its officers. However, he admired greatly the tenacity, stoicism and heroism of the Ottoman soldiers. (AWM, J00200)

von Sanders made minor changes to the defensive plans, which actually dated back to Kemal's service on the peninsula in the First Balkan War in 1913. Important to this narrative, on 7 April he designated Kemal's division as the Fifth Army reserve and moved it north from Eceabat to an assembly area centred on the tiny village of Bigalı. Meeting Liman von Sanders for the first time Kemal was asked whether he believed the Germans would win the war to which, unsurprisingly, he replied that he was not yet convinced they would. Nevertheless Kemal, his chief of staff Major Izzettin (later Çalışlar), and his regimental commanders feverishly trained their men for war with intensive live-firing exercises, long and rapid road marches, and combat drill rehearsals.

Ottoman intelligence believed that 70,000 Allied soldiers were poised to descend on the peninsula and, indeed, they were. The Ottomans knew they were coming and continuously rehearsed their anti-invasion plans and drills. What they did not know was the exact time of the landings or the precise points at which the Allies would land. As a result the Fifth Army put light forces guarding the beaches and positioned heavy reserves behind them with the idea of massing their forces once the actual landings had been identified. As the Fifth Army reserve, Kemal's division was poised to move in any direction at a moment's notice. In the words of the famous Canadian World War I Ace Billy Bishop, VC, 'on the edge of destiny you must test your strength' and as late April 1915 approached Lieutenant-Colonel Mustafa Kemal and his 19th Infantry Division stood on the edge of destiny.

THE HOUR OF DESTINY

It is difficult and probably incorrect to identify a particular hour of destiny for Mustafa Kemal. He is most well known for his decisive counterattacks on the Australian and New Zealand Army Corps (ANZAC) at Gallipoli on 25 April 1915. However, later in the campaign he commanded a corps-sized tactical group that played an equally decisive role in stopping the second British attack at Suvla Bay. In fact, it was Kemal's actions in the Suvla battles (or Anafarta battles as they are known in Turkey) of 9–28 August 1915, which brought him to the notice of the Ottoman public. Later in the war, in Syria, his command of the Ottoman Seventh Army's retreat after the defeat at Megiddo in September 1918 was arguably his greatest military achievement. Moreover, in 1922 during the Turkish War of Independence, Kemal's reconstitution of the nationalist army and his brilliant encirclement campaign known as 'The Great Offensive' stand out dramatically as well. This section will, therefore, look at four particular decisive points in Kemal's career – as a lieutenant-colonel commanding a division, as a colonel commanding a corps-level group, as a major-general commanding an army and as a field marshal commanding an army group.

Man of destiny

Lieutenant-Colonel Mustafa Kemal (1), in command of an Ottoman infantry division, in front of his headquarters in the small village of Bigalı with his aide-de-camp (2) at 7am, 25 April 1915. He has alerted and readied the regiments of the 19th Infantry Division to meet the invading Australians. Two soldiers from the 57th Infantry Regiment (3), Kemal's best unit and the first regiment he will launch that day, stand ready to march along the circuitous route leading to the ANZAC beachhead. Today the Bigalı house (4) is a museum.

Kemal arrived on the high ground overlooking the beaches around mid-morning to find the Australians swarming up the heights. He rallied the retreating Ottoman soldiers and reinforced them with his own 57th Regiment. It was here that Kemal gave his famous command, 'I don't order you to attack, I order you to die ... and, in that time, others will come up to take our places'. Kemal went on to organize a series of powerful infantry and artillery attacks that rocked the Australians and collapsed their morale. His attacks were so fierce that, late that night, Lieutenant-General Sir William Birdwood, commander of the ANZAC, asked General Sir Ian Hamilton for permission to withdraw the landing force, to which Hamilton famously told the Australians to stay put and 'to dig, dig, dig'. As the day passed, Liman von Sanders appointed Kemal as the Ari Burnu (ANZAC Beach) front commander with unitary command over the Ottoman units containing the ANZACs. Within a week, Kemal had command of the major elements of four infantry divisions, nearly succeeding in throwing the Australians back into the sea before the situation stabilized. Kemal's performance in command of large forces in desperate circumstances established his reputation as a combat leader and solidified the confidence of General Otto Liman von Sanders in his abilities.

Division and group command

The massive Allied invasion of the Gallipoli peninsula began about an hour before dawn on 25 April 1915 when the British landed at Cape Helles on the tip of the peninsula and the Australians landed at what would become known as ANZAC Beach in the middle of the peninsula. These landings occurred in the 9th Infantry Division's sector of the III Corps area of responsibility. Central to the division's plan was the position of Lieutenant-Colonel Şefik's 27th Infantry Regiment in reserve near Eceabat. Alerted to the landings at ANZAC Beach, Şefik ordered his two battalions forward about 6am to counterattack the invaders. By 8.30am his men were firmly in contact with the advancing elements of the 1st Australian Infantry Division.

By coincidence, Kemal was up early that morning preparing the 57th Infantry Regiment for training and the regiment was preparing for movement. Receiving the landing reports he alerted his entire division at 5.30am and ordered his cavalry detachment to reconnoitre the routes to Koja Chemen Tepe, a key hill overlooking the ANZAC landings. Kemal impatiently awaited orders but none came. At 7am, on his own initiative, he ordered the 57th Infantry Regiment, an artillery battery and his medical detachment to follow the cavalry routes forward and he notified the III Corps commander of his actions. Kemal and his aide-de-camp also went forward. Alerted by III Corps that Kemal was moving into his sector, the 9th Infantry Division commander ordered Şefik to coordinate his counterattack with the 19th Infantry Division. Kemal arrived on Chunuk Bair about 9.40am and immediately energized the faltering defence. Famously, he ordered men who were out of ammunition for their rifles to fix bayonets and await the enemy's attack. As his own 57th Infantry Regiment began to arrive, Kemal coordinated a combined attack with the 27th Infantry Regiment. It was at this moment when Kemal famously told his men, 'I'm not ordering you to attack... I'm ordering you to die.' About 12.30pm, both regiments went forward in a carefully orchestrated hasty counter-attack ('hasty' is a doctrinal term meaning an operation which is extemporaneously planned and is unrehearsed. The opposite doctrinal term is a 'deliberate' operation) supported by artillery and machine guns. Although outnumbered, the fresh Ottomans hit the Australians, who were

19th Infantry Division, Gallipoli, 25 April 1917

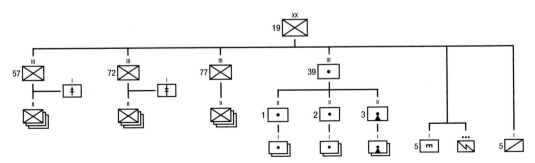

exhausted and badly positioned to repel an attack. The concentration of Kemal and Şefik's combat power shattered the Australians and rocked their confidence levels. Importantly, it brought their advance to a halt and proved decisive in holding the enemy to a small perimeter.

As the day progressed, Kemal ordered his other regiments forward to contain the expanding ANZAC perimeter completely. His prescient decision to move his regiments without orders was vindicated when Esat Pasha, III Corps commander, confirmed his decisions and appointed him as the Ari Burnu (ANZAC) Front Commander in the early afternoon, charging Kemal with tactical responsibility for the entire ANZAC beachhead. Esat also transferred the 9th Infantry Division's 27th Infantry Regiment to Kemal's command as well. In the late afternoon and evening Kemal attacked with his fresh 72nd and 77th Infantry Regiments and, by midnight, Lieutenant-General William Birdwood, the ANZAC commander, and his two division commanders were urgently pleading to be withdrawn from the beaches. Sir Ian Hamilton, the British commander of the Mediterranean Expeditionary Force, refused their requests and ordered them instead to stay put and 'dig, dig, dig'. Over the next several days, Liman von Sanders sent six additional infantry regiments with artillery to reinforce Kemal, who launched a series of violent counterattacks. Although unsuccessful these attacks successfully compressed the ANZACs into a small and vulnerable perimeter with Kemal commanding the high ground. Altogether, he commanded the equivalent of several infantry divisions with his tiny divisional headquarters. On 29 April 1915, Esat Pasha was designated as the Northern Group commander and Kemal returned to division-level command.

Esat Pasha in an artillery position during the Gallipoli campaign in 1915. Esat was rather grandfatherly in appearance yet that belied his tactical skills as a proven combat leader. In battle, he was decisive and able to bring combat power to the critical point. After Gallipoli, Esat would go on to command Third Army in the Caucasus. (ATASE)

Enver Pasha graduated from the Ottoman War Academy in 1903 and moved upward at an astonishing rate. In January 1914 he was appointed as the Ottoman Minister of War. He was charismatic, brilliant, but often reckless in his decision-making. (AWM, H12357)

Using fresh reinforcements Enver Pasha directed the Fifth Army make a maximum effort to crush the ANZAC beachhead. In turn, the Northern Group commander Esat planned a massive four-division night attack for 19 May. Launched one hour before dawn, the attack was a monumental disaster because the ANZACs had detected it and were wide awake and ready. Of note is Kemal's carefully crafted order and professional execution, which

The ANZAC perimeter, 19 May 1915

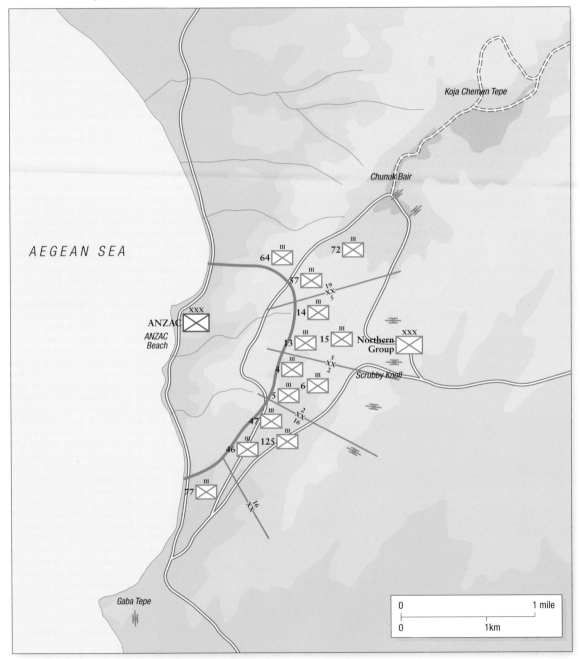

Mustafa Kemal's counter-attack, 9 August 1915

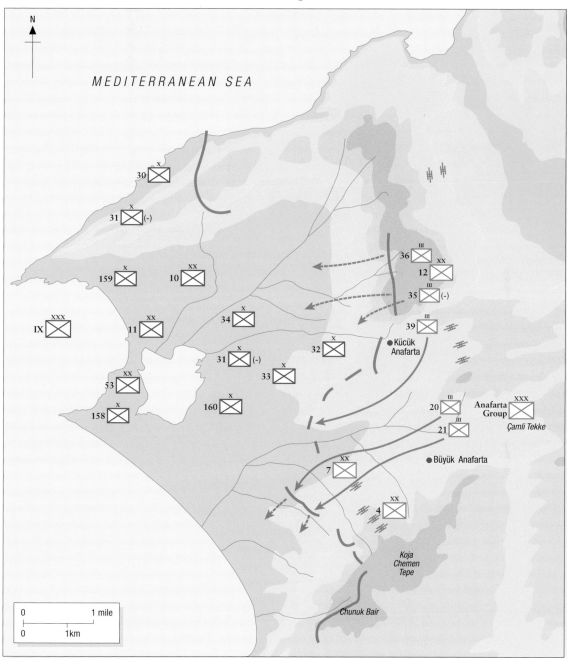

resulted in the 19th Infantry Division suffering the lowest casualty rates of the four participating infantry divisions. In recognition of Kemal's brilliant combat performance, Liman von Sanders awarded him the Iron Cross on 23 May and he was also promoted to colonel (*albay*) on 1 June 1915.

Kemal's division held the northern sector of the Ottoman position and he was concerned about its almost undefended right flank. Typically, he sent

The 19th Division staff. Ottoman infantry division staffs were tiny in comparison with western Allied staffs. A typical Ottoman division staff comprised about a dozen officers compared with over 70 officers on a British division staff. (Mesut Uyar)

repeated warnings to Esat. Finally, an irritated Esat came down in mid-June to examine personally the disputed terrain in what is known as the 'Sazlıdere Discussion'. Kemal pointed out the gap in the defences and vigorously advanced his ideas noting that the enemy might swing a major force up and over the unguarded Koja Chemen Tepe (or Chunuk Bair) thus flanking the Northern Group. Esat and his chief of staff rejected Kemal's analysis as impracticable and left the position as it was with only observation posts on the high ground. This would prove to be a near-fatal tactical mistake.

Faced with a Western Front-style stalemate, the British decided to conduct a major flanking attack in conjunction with a supporting amphibious assault to break the deadlock at Gallipoli. On 6 August 1915, the ANZACs, supported by X Army Corps, launched an attack exactly where Kemal had predicted it would come. Often known collectively today as 'Suvla Bay' the Turks know these battles today as Anafarta and Conkbayırı with the main British attack aimed at seizing the highest point in the peninsula at Chunuk Bair. The Allied plan went quickly awry because of incredibly bad leadership in X Corps and through bad planning assumptions by the ANZACs. This was matched by confused command relationships on the Ottoman side, which led to a delay in the arrival of reinforcements. To rectify this, an anxious Liman von Sanders placed Kemal in command of the newly formed six-division Anafarta Group on 8 August.

Officially, although still a colonel, Kemal was now a corps-level commander. Kemal immediately consolidated the defence and launched a powerful counter-attack, which he led in person, dislodging the enemy from their positions. Famously, he was hit in the chest by shrapnel on 10 August, which was deflected by his pocket watch. Unfazed by this he coolly continued in command without pause. He stabilized the situation, which once again returned the Ottoman front to a defensive posture, after which he presented his damaged watch to Liman von Sanders as a keepsake.

The Allies were unable to break through the Ottoman lines and were faced with increasing their troop levels. Convinced that the campaign was unwinnable, the British decided to withdraw and completed their evacuation of the peninsula in early January 1916. Kemal did not witness the withdrawal because he was medically evacuated for exhaustion in November, but he emerged from the campaign with a proven record as a courageous and decisive corps-level commander.

Kemal took command of XVI Army Corps in Edirne on 27 January 1916, which was in turn ordered to the Caucasian front in March. He arrived in the south-eastern Anatolian city of Diyarbakır on 27 March and was promoted to major-general (*tümgeneral*) on 1 April 1916. His corps slowly arrived over the empire's antique lines of communications and it was not until mid-summer that his corps was in the line near Lake Van. In the Ottoman Second Army's summer offensive, XVI Corps drove towards and seized the city of Muş. Kemal's operations were well planned and were marked by extremely fast tactical movements by his infantry. Soon Bitlis fell to Kemal's forces as well. Flawed inter-army coordination doomed the offensive, which ground to a halt in late summer. Kemal was assigned to command the entire Second Army in October 1916 and then presided over a very quiet situation as both sides tried to replace their losses over the coming winter and spring.

Army command

In late June 1917, Kemal attended a high-level strategy meeting in Aleppo at which Enver unveiled his plans to form a joint German–Ottoman army group to retake Baghdad in a major offensive operation. Command of the new army group was given to German General Erich von Falkenhayn. Enver also offered Kemal command of the new Ottoman Seventh Army, then forming near Damascus, and which was slated as a component of the new army group. Kemal accepted and took up the command on 8 August. Politics now intervened again in Kemal's career as Cemal, Falkenhayn and Enver began to argue over whether the Seventh Army should deploy to Baghdad or to the badly threatened Sinai front in Palestine. Of course, Kemal could be counted on to weigh in with his opinions, which he did and which turned out to be serious criticisms of the basic war strategy itself.

Colonel Mustafa Kemal, sometime in August 1915 as commander of the Anafarta Group, gazing towards the enemy positions. This iconic photo, showing the intensity level of a combat commander literally leaning forward into the enemy, is one of the most beloved and popular images of Atatürk in Turkey today. (AWM, A05319)

A junior officer reports to an obviously weary Colonel Mustafa Kemal during the Gallipoli Campaign. Kemal wears the distinctive cap, the Enveriye, named after Enver Pasha who personally designed it, and riding boots. (AWM, A05288)

23

On 20 September 1917, Kemal sent copies of an unsolicited report he had written to Enver, Talât (then the interior minister) and the grand vizier expressing his concerns about the faltering Ottoman war effort. Kemal began by pointing out the unfavourable strategic situation and blamed it primarily on the Germans. He then advanced the idea that the Ottomans should give up all offensive operations (such as the Baghdad offensive) and posture the empire on the strategic defensive. He continued saying, rather than squander increasingly scarce resources in fruitless attacks, that all surplus troop units should be held in reserve to be committed to halting major Allied offensives. Additionally, Kemal recommended that Germans be removed from most command positions because he believed they were using the Ottomans for their own self-serving interests. Kemal ended with the recommendation that the high command send his Seventh Army to the Sinai to assist in the defence of Palestine rather than to retake Baghdad. This was a singularly blunt criticism of the offensive strategic thinking of Enver, who was the

Enver Pasha decorating one of Kemal's officers; Kemal is standing to the right. In spite of personal antagonisms and repeated public criticism by Kemal of his strategic policies, Enver recognized Kemal's talent and value to the war effort. (Mesut Uyar)

Kemal in command

Colonel Mustafa Kemal in the trenches, 6 August 1915. Kemal observes the British advance from Suvla Bay toward the sector of his 19th Division on Conkbayırı Ridge. Two days later, the Ottoman Fifth Army commander, General Otto Liman von Sanders, would appoint Kemal as commander of the newly formed Anafarta Group replacing a failing commander. Given the task of containing the Allied offensive Kemal once again stabilized the defence and launched powerful counterattacks to stop the advancing British. On 10 August, Kemal crept forward into no man's land to lead personally the devastating counterattack on Chunuk Bair that swept the enemy off the Farm Plateau. Famously, when shrapnel hit him in the chest, shattering his watch but saving his life, he shouted to those who had seen him hit, 'Silence, Don't let the men lose their morale!' Later he presented the broken watch to Liman von Sanders as a keepsake.

By the middle of August, Kemal's group would swell in size to include seven infantry divisions and a number of attached regiments. In effect, the Anafarta Group was a small army rather than a large corps. By September 1915, Kemal's sector had lapsed into stasis and the stagnation of trench warfare asserted itself. Over seven months of heavy and sustained combat took their toll even on the seemingly invulnerable Kemal and, exhausted and sick, he was evacuated from the peninsula to hospital on 10 December.

Kemal's consistent and capable command of Ottoman forces on the Gallipoli peninsula marked him for more responsibility and for high command. He would move up rapidly in 1916 to corps command and in 1917 to field army level command.

General Otto Liman von Sanders, commander of the Yildirim Army Group in Palestine sometime in 1918. He appears to be discussing a military exercise with a naval officer while Ottoman officials and Austro-Hungarian officers listen to his comments. (AWM, H13382)

Minister of War, and a brutal condemnation of the empire's German ally. Moreover, Kemal could not resist exchanging angry letters with Falkenhayn, in which he expressed the same concerns. Of course, all of this brought a scathing rebuke from Enver and Kemal resigned his command on 4 October. Never one to take affront lying down, Kemal took leave in Istanbul and continued his public criticism of the war effort over the following winter. Unsurprisingly, and despite lobbying for a new command, he remained unemployed by the army. Depressed by inactivity and suffering from kidney problems he applied for medical leave to take a cure in Austria–Hungary and spent two months in Karlsbad.

Kemal was not to be sidelined for very long. The newly enthroned Ottoman Sultan, Vahdettin – who took the name Mehmet VI – was an admirer of Kemal's and was responsible for his rehabilitation to active service. The operational and tactical situation in Palestine in the summer of 1918 can only be described as desperate and Mehmet VI asked that Kemal be reappointed to command the Seventh Army, which had been sent to Syria rather than to Baghdad. Enver relented and Kemal took command of the army on 7 August 1918. The Seventh Army was one of three field armies assigned to the Yildirim Army Group, which was now under the command of Kemal's former commander at Gallipoli, German General Liman von Sanders. On paper, the army was a powerful military instrument composed of two army corps each having two infantry divisions and corps artillery assigned. Kemal's two corps commanders were his friends, Ali Fuat and İsmet (later İnönü), who were experienced and trusted subordinates. However, the Palestine front was starved of men, supplies and equipment and, although his army was authorized over 60,000 men, Kemal found the Seventh Army had less than 20,000 men assigned, of whom only 7,000 were infantrymen. Moreover, the men were malnourished and the draft animals upon which tactical movement depended were badly undernourished as well. Moreover, the army group tasked the Seventh Army to hold an extended front and then failed to provide the engineer materials necessary to adequately fortify the trenches.

On 19 September 1918, the commander of the British Egyptian Expeditionary Force, General Sir Edmund Allenby, launched his long-awaited offensive in Palestine. Known in Britain as the battle of Megiddo, Allenby intended to break through the Ottoman lines and conduct a cavalry encirclement campaign of annihilation. Allenby's army struck the Ottoman Eighth Army's XXII Army Corps, on the far right flank adjacent to the Mediterranean coast, with a 12 to one superiority in men and a four to one superiority in artillery. The attack began at dawn and

Yildirim Army Group, Palestine, late September 1918

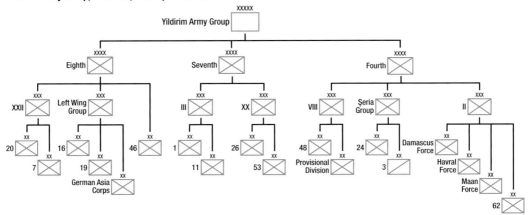

within two hours Allenby's army completely ruptured the Eighth Army's lines and had drawn in all of its available reserves. In his memoirs, Liman von Sanders reckoned that by 7am the Eighth Army ceased to exist as a fighting force. Allenby then unleashed his Cavalry Corps of three full cavalry divisions through the gap with orders to drive on the town of Nablus, where Kemal's Seventh Army headquarters was located, and encircle the enemy.

The Ottoman commanders were not surprised by Allenby's deception operations in the Jordan River valley and were expecting a major British offensive in the Eighth Army sector. Thus, Kemal was not surprised when British aircraft bombed his headquarters at 5am on 19 September, knocking out his telephone lines. Shortly thereafter, the British hit İsmet's III Corps with a supporting attack but there was little real pressure in Kemal's sector.

The next day, Kemal was able to shift several battalions from his XX Corps to reinforce III Corps. Although his own lines were holding, Kemal was forced to react to the massive cavalry and infantry force threatening to envelop his right flank. He notified his commanders that he intended to pull back off the defensive line and move north. He had III Corps block the enemy while XX Corps broke contact and withdrew. The news of the Eighth Army's catastrophic defeat rapidly spread throughout the Seventh Army and Kemal had difficulty maintaining morale. Nevertheless, Kemal withdrew his army in good order and began to move it northeast to Biesan. Unfortunately, Allenby's rapidly moving cavalry beat him there and crossed the Jordan River blocking his retreat.

From his headquarters in Beyti Hasan, Kemal reacted equally swiftly and ordered his units due east to cross the river. With the remnants of the Eighth Army to his north most of Kemal's forces made it safely across the Jordan River on the night of 23/24 September. Relentlessly pursued by the enemy, Kemal slowed the British with a

İsmet İnönü graduated from the Ottoman War Academy in 1906. He served as a corps and army commander and retired from the Turkish army in 1927. He served as president of the Republic from 1938 to 1950 and in the early 1960s as prime minister. (Mesut Uyar)

The Seventh Army retreat from Megiddo, 19 September to 28 October 1918

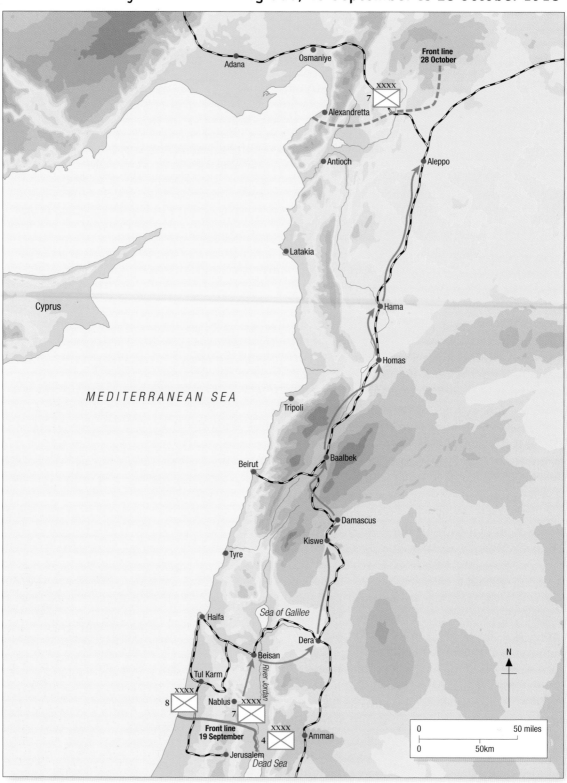

Adana

Osmaniye

XXXX
7

Front line
28 October

Alexandretta

Antioch

Aleppo

Latakia

Hama

Homas

MEDITERRANEAN SEA

Cyprus

Tripoli

Beirut

Baalbek

Damascus

Kiswe

Tyre

Haifa

Sea of Galilee

Dera

Beisan

River Jordan

Tul Karm

XXXX
8

Nablus

XXXX
7

Front line
19 September

XXXX
4

Amman

Jerusalem

Dead Sea

N

0   50 miles

0   50km

screening operation conducted by the 3rd Cavalry Division, while he withdrew the Seventh Army to Dera on 27 September. In the meantime, Indian and Australian cavalry were racing up the coast to the west towards Damascus and the Arabs launched minor attacks on the Hedjaz railway. Alert to the fact that the capture of Damascus would trap almost the entire army group, Liman von Sanders ordered Kemal to move formations to blocking positions south-west of the city. Marching rapidly north for two days, İsmet's III Corps reached Kisve Station on the outskirts of Damascus on 30 September, pivoting west just in time to establish a thin defensive line. This halted the advancing enemy cavalry. Kemal positioned the 3rd Cavalry Division on İsmet's left flank and used Ali Fuat's XX Corps to block the Arabs, hoping to hold the escape route open long enough to withdraw his forces. The remnants of the Fourth and Eighth Armies followed and most successfully moved though Damascus. However, the British pushed Kemal's battered forces back and entered Damascus on 1 October. Kemal's shattered 26th and 53rd Infantry Divisions, as well as the 3rd Cavalry Division, were trapped and forced to surrender. Although the Seventh Army lost some its fighting formations, this difficult defensive manoeuvre arguably saved the surviving bulk of the Yildirim Army Group from certain extinction

Kemal now fell back on the railway to Baalbeck with XX Corps, which he reconstituted using the 24th and 43rd Infantry Divisions, while III Corps blocked the roads north at Eski Han. To their rear the Fourth Army organized the defence of Homs. This was an important geographic location because it was the convergence point for the avenues of advance north into Syria as the coast lacked good roads. Although the British took Homs on 3 October their progress north now slowed to a crawl. Kemal now pulled his battered army north to Aleppo, while the Fourth Army delayed the enemy at Homs, which fell six days later. Kemal's small army still contained III Corps and XX Corps and he set to work in an attempt to defend Aleppo and established a defensive line south-west of the city.

On 20 October, Kemal reorganized his command structure again by assigning the 1st and 11th Infantry Divisions to Ali Fuat's XX Corps. He tasked İsmet with reconstituting III Corps and assigned him the 24th and 43rd Infantry Divisions. Kemal assigned the defence of Aleppo to XX Corps, which contained veteran and trusted infantry divisions. Although the city's defences were weak, the British chose not to assault Kemal's lines frontally and British cavalry swept to the north-west of Aleppo in an attempt to envelop the city on 26 October. According to the British official history Kemal

Ottoman artillery battery in Palestine. Ottoman artillery batteries were assigned four guns or howitzers. The commander and his observation party are on the left. (Mesut Uyar)

Allied ships steaming toward Istanbul's Golden Horn. After the armistice the Allied navies, led by the Royal Navy's HMS *Superb*, paraded through the Dardanelles on 12 November 1918 and anchored off Istanbul the next day. What force of arms did not accomplish during the Gallipoli Campaign was finally achieved. (AWM, H18875)

came up in person and directed a vigorous blocking operation with great boldness. However, his forces were too small and enemy cavalry seized Aleppo at 10am that day. Fortunately Kemal was able to withdraw his army from the city. By this time, the battered Fourth Army had collapsed entirely leaving Kemal's Seventh Army as the sole survivor of three Ottoman armies which were stationed in Palestine on 19 September.

Pulling out of Aleppo Kemal re-established his headquarters at Katma and withdrew using XX Corps' divisions to maintain contact with the enemy. The indefatigable Kemal moved his headquarters to Raco and began to prepare yet another defensive line along what is now the southern border of Turkey. Behind him lay the Ottoman Second Army guarding the coast and the city of Adana and forces from it were assigned to reinforce him. However, before Allenby could marshal an attack on the Anatolian heartland, the Ottoman Empire negotiated an armistice on 30 October which brought the war to a close. Germany immediately recalled Liman von Sanders and Mustafa Kemal briefly assumed command of the front. The Yildirim Army Group and Seventh Army were dissolved on 7 November 1918 and Kemal remained in command of the Second Army.

A successful retreat while aggressively pursued by a more mobile enemy is one of the most difficult military operations imaginable. It is rarely seen in military history and many historians consider the successful execution of this operation as a signature hallmark of a great general. Of note is the astounding control that Kemal exercised over his army in almost impossible circumstances at the end of which he still maintained a coherent and combat capable force.

Kemal, the armistice and nationalism

Kemal was one of a number of professional military officers who have come to be known in Turkish history as 'the nationalist group of officers'. When it became clear that World War I would end in the defeat of Germany and the Ottoman Empire they became politically active with a view towards preserving the independence and territorial integrity of a Turkish successor state. In the summer of 1918, Kemal was in contact with a number of these officers, including Fethi (Okyar) and Rauf (Orbay), who were conspiring to replace the CUP government. Kemal hoped to be appointed minister of war in a new government.

Throughout his service in the retreat to Aleppo, Kemal remained in contact with his friends and maintained a constant finger on the pulse of the political affairs in Istanbul. However, he was still deeply engaged in the military campaign when the CUP cabinet collapsed on 10 October and retired general Ahmet İzzet formed a new government as prime minister. Kemal pressed his associates hard and tried unsuccessfully to secure a place for himself in the new government. Although Rauf secured a cabinet post, the nationalists were unable to convince Izzet not to approve the Allies' armistice agreement. When he received the full text of the armistice on 3 November 1918, Kemal was furious with the terms, which turned over control of such key strategic locations as Istanbul, the Dardanelles, the Pozanti tunnel and Mosul to the Allies. This caused him to send telegrams to the capital opposing certain clauses of the armistice and stating that he intended to oppose the British occupation of Iskenderun by force. Izzet ordered him to peacefully turn over the city and then promptly resigned as prime minister – but not before relieving Kemal of his post. On 10 November 1918, Kemal turned over command of the Second Army and departed for the capital by train from Adana. He arrived in Istanbul three days later to find the Allied fleet anchored in the city's Golden Horn. Once again, Kemal now found himself still in the army but without a command.

Within a short period of time, the Allies occupied the capital, the straits and most of Cilicia and set about supervising the demobilization of the Ottoman army. Under the terms of the armistice, the army was reduced to 20 very under-strength infantry divisions, totalling less than 50,000 men, and very small amounts of equipment. Subsequently, the Versailles peace settlement in 1919 divested the Ottoman Empire of its Middle Eastern provinces (Arabia, Yemen, Iraq, Lebanon, Palestine and Syria) leaving it with what was essentially the mostly Turkish heartland of Anatolia. Moreover, a succession of ineffective cabinets was unable to prevent the Italians, Greeks and Armenians from occupying even more parts of Anatolia than the victors anticipated. As a result, resistance from the group of nationalist officers to this piecemeal destruction of the country began almost immediately after the first days of occupation.

In Istanbul, Kemal continued his political machinations but he was unsuccessful in advancing himself for a command or key staff position. Likewise, he was unable to generate much government support for his cause of halting foreign intervention and ejecting foreign forces from the territory remaining to the empire. At the same time, the hunt for, and imprisonment of, former CUP leaders, who were now considered war criminals, began in earnest in early 1919 as the Ottoman government sought to appease the Allies regarding the Armenian massacres and the ill-treatment of prisoners of war. Several of Kemal's

Kemal stands with a regimental colour bearer directly behind him. The regiments and divisions of the former Ottoman army, which went over to the nationalists, retained their numbers, colours, lineages and traditions in the Turkish army. (Mesut Uyar)

erstwhile political and military associates were arrested but he was not. Whether the Allies wanted him arrested is unclear and, even though he was an ardent CUP member and nationalist, Kemal's name is not associated today with any of the war's excesses.

Beyond securing the war minister's portfolio in the government for himself, Kemal's most compelling concern was the ongoing demobilization of the Ottoman Army. In the spring of 1919, Allied control commission officers, the most aggressive of which were British, fanned out across the truncated empire to count and collect weapons for demilitarization. Kemal was encouraged when the government appointed a number of nationalist officers to command important formations of the army, including Fahrettin (Altay) in XII Corps in Konya, Ali Fuat (Cebesoy) in III Corps in Ankara and Kâzım Karabekir in XV Corps in Erzurum. All of these men had served at Gallipoli with Kemal and they commanded some of the largest formations remaining in the armistice army. Moreover, the government gave his friend Refet (Bele) command over the Ottoman gendarmerie, a large and well-trained paramilitary force, stationed throughout the empire's cities and towns. According to one historian, Kemal, Rauf and these officers were 'the original military planners of the Turkish War of Independence'. In addition, his former comrade-in-arms İsmet was a frequent visitor at Kemal's house and also helped formulate a plan of action.

Karabekir left for the east determined to hold back the advancing Armenians, while the others took up their posts equally determined to conceal weapons from the Allied inspectors. They were taking their lives in their own hands since the Sultan went to any lengths to please the Allies and their actions effectively made them criminals. In March 1919, the Italians seized the Mediterranean port city of Antalya, while the Hellenic government announced claims to Izmir and its hinterlands, as well as to the Pontus region of the Black Sea coast. Kemal continued to lobby for active service or a position in government. Finally, on 9 April 1919, he was appointed Ninth Army Inspector, which in the German-derived peacetime Ottoman command architecture effectively amounted to the position of army commander. This was no small success for Kemal as the Ninth Army contained Karabekir's XV Corps of four infantry divisions and Ali Fuat's III Corps of two infantry divisions.

Throughout this period, Kemal had extensive meetings with Fevzi (Çakmak) the outgoing chief of the general staff and his successor Cevat (Çobanlı), who were nationalists themselves and clandestinely supportive of what Kemal wanted to

Kemal in the winter on the Anatolian front. The winter weather on the high plateau of Anatolia is often below freezing making military operation arduous and difficult. A lack of trees for firewood and a lack of coal not only affected individual soldiers but also impeded the operations of the few steam locomotives in the hands of the nationalists. (Mesut Uyar)

accomplish. On 15 May, while Kemal was still in Istanbul, the Hellenic army landed in Izmir with the intent of annexing it. This was a surprise to the government, which had not taken seriously Greek Prime Minister Venizelos' *Megáli Idéa* (or Great Idea), which advanced the notion that a greater modern Greece must encircle the Aegean Sea and include Istanbul as well as ancient Ionia (the eastern Aegean littoral and most of western Anatolia).

On 16 May 1919, Kemal boarded the elderly steamer *Bandirma* bound for Samsun on the Black Sea coast. The British inspectors searched the ship before its departure looking for weapons and contraband. Kemal exclaimed during the inspection, 'We are not taking contraband or arms, but faith and determination'. Kemal and his personal staff landed in Samsun on 19 May, which has been celebrated as a national holiday since 1935, and initiated a campaign to unite the disjointed nationalist resistance movement. Belatedly, that day, the British asked why the government was sending a man to command the Ninth Army, a field army that was, itself, designated for demobilization. British inspectors in Samsun were alerted to closely monitor Kemal's actions and warned him repeatedly and strongly about supporting anti-government nationalist groups. Undeterred by these admonitions, Kemal left the city several days later after stirring up anti-Greek sentiment bound for the interior. Kemal then visited army and gendarmerie garrisons and sent telegraph messages to all army headquarters urging commanders to demand independence from foreign occupation. Encouraged by Kemal's proclamations nationalist protest groups formed in the empire's cities, often coalescing around military commanders and units. Kemal then appointed himself as the Inspector of the Ottoman Third Army. Kemal's provocative actions immediately caused the British to demand his relief and the government consequently forbade the telegraph transmission of nationalist messages encouraging resistance.

Most telegraph officials ignored the government's directive and Kemal was able to send his Amasya Circular on 21/22 June explaining the need for a national parliamentary body and giving notice to hold a 'national congress' in Sivas. In fact, provisional nationalist congresses were already in existence in a number of provinces and cities already. Kemal's signature on the circular was essentially an act of open rebellion against the Ottoman government. It also brought him into conflict with Karabekir, who thought his actions were too strong. The government's reaction was conflicted with only the interior minister demanding his return to Istanbul.

Kemal went to Erzurum where he sent out his last telegraph message that army formations should not demobilize further and that no more arms or munitions should be handed over to the Allies. This action proved too much for the Sultan's government and provoked a strong response from Istanbul. On the night of 8/9 July 1919, Kemal traded angry telegrams with the minister of war, at the end of which Kemal tendered his resignation from the army. It was not immediately clear what would happen next but Karabekir was appointed to replace Kemal, though he refused to alter the basic tenets of Kemal's directives. At the same time, Refet also tendered his resignation

Kemal exiting the Western Front headquarters in 1922. Kemal was an activist commander-in-chief and often visited the army headquarters on the Greek front. He personally checked all major operational plans for both conceptual design and completeness of preparations. (Mesut Uyar)

from the army and, on 23 July, the regional Erzurum Congress opened to elect delegates to send to Sivas, at which the nationalists planned to convene a national congress. Still wearing his uniform and supported by Karabekir, Kemal wrangled politically with the Trabzon representatives but finally prevailed to lead the delegation destined for the congress in Sivas. More importantly, a political doctrine was drawn up that rejected the dismemberment of the empire by foreign occupation and affirmed that the army was responsible for its territorial integrity. In the meantime, Greek forces encircled Izmir and began to push into the interior.

The Sivas Congress opened on 4 September 1919. The government ordered Kemal's arrest and sent a troop of Kurdish cavalry to apprehend him. Kemal received warnings and an Ottoman cavalry detachment successfully intercepted the Kurds. This enabled Kemal to convince many of the delegates at the congress to reach a nationalist consensus, which adopted the ideas of the Erzurum Congress. Again the government responded weakly with a conflicted response that seemed to embrace the nationalist positions. In the end, the Sivas Congress was something of a declaration of war on foreign occupation of Anatolia and European Turkey. The last Ottoman parliament convened in January 1920 and affirmed the nationalist position thus enraging the British, who immediately established a caretaker puppet government. This ill-founded move drove many fence sitters into the arms of the nationalists and many fled subsequently into the interior to join Kemal. On 19 March 1920, Kemal announced that the Turkish nation was establishing its own parliament in Ankara under the name Grand National Assembly. On 23 April, with 100 members from the Ottoman parliament who had escaped from Istanbul and 190 elected delegates from around the country, the new national assembly convened for the first time. The following day, the assembly immediately elected Kemal as the first president and İsmet as the army's chief of staff. Fevzi was later reappointed minister of war in the nationalist cabinet and the army went over to the nationalist cause. What the Turks call the Turkish War of Independence (*Türk Milli Mücadele*) was about to begin.

Commander-in-chief

The spring and summer of 1920 were difficult times for the nationalists. At the San Remo Conference, 19–26 April, the Allies finalized their mandate system and authorized the Greek occupation of Aydin province and eastern Thrace. There was a civil war going on between a number of private armies in Anatolia, which included renegade nationalists and Kurdish chieftains. The Circassian rebel leaders, Çerkes Ethem and Ahmet Anzavur, fought both the Greeks and the new Ankara government. Making things worse, Armenians were raiding over the eastern border and trying to reclaim the areas around Erzurum. The Hellenic army occupying Izmir launched a serious offensive on 22 June aimed at expanding their bridgehead, and took Bandirma and Bursa in July. They also occupied Thrace, forcing the surrender of the Edirne garrison. On 10 August 1920, the Allies concluded the Treaty of Sèvres which, in addition to ratifying the San Remo decisions, gave the Aegean islands and Izmir to Greece, allowed for the establishment of Kurdistan in south-eastern Turkey and demilitarized the Dardanelles straits. The Sultan's rump government signed the treaty while the Ankara assembly declared those who signed it were traitors to the empire. Above all, the treaty energized the Greeks to renew their offensive operations.

Kemal was besieged with internal and external crises. He reacted with typical alacrity and set to dealing with these problems one by one. He sent an ambassador to Moscow to ask for weapons to fight the western imperialists, which began to arrive later that year. Kemal sent the army to crush the Circassian rebels. He appointed Karabekir commander of the Eastern Front on 15 June to deal with the Armenians and then appointed Ali Fuat commander of the Western Front facing the Greeks. When the Allies broke up the nationalist groups in Istanbul, Kemal founded and organized the remaining civil servants into a nationwide organization called the National Defence Organization and charged it with re-energising public support for the Ankara government using the telegraph and postal systems. While accomplishing all of this, Kemal also began to move army units to Ankara to refit and retrain them.

Arms and equipment remained a constant problem for the nationalists. Surprising many people, and especially the British, Kemal brokered a deal with the new Soviet state for the purchase of military weapons. Altogether, in the name of 'anti-imperialism,' the Soviets provided the nationalists with 45,000 rifles, 300 machine guns, a hundred artillery pieces and tons of ammunition. Ironically, much of this came from captured stocks destined for the Tsar that were abandoned by the Allies. There were other sources of weapons as well from demobilizing but impoverished European countries hungry for cash. For example, Germany sold the nationalists 10,000 rifles, 5,000 swords, 1,000 Parabellum pistols, 26 aircraft, 500km of telephone cable, 100,000 hand grenades and many other military supplies. Even the French, who were technically allied with Greece against the nationalists and were actually occupying southern Cilicia, sold the Turks weapons, including 1,500 light machine guns, ten aircraft and tons of ammunition.

By October 1920, the nationalist army had coalesced into an effectively organized and well-led force, although it remained greatly understrength. Kemal maintained a 'frontal' system of command rather than designate forces as numbered field armies, which effectively endowed subordinate commanders with independence of command. Faced with a renewal of a

Greek offensive that month, Kemal relieved Ali Fuat, in whom he had lost confidence, and replaced him with İsmet. He then divided the Greek front into Western and Southern sectors and retained İsmet as Western Front commander. Refet was appointed as Southern Front commander in Konya. Altogether, the nationalist army comprised 19 infantry divisions and one cavalry division and Kemal was reactivating an additional infantry division and two mounted infantry divisions as well. In the east, Karabekir commanded four infantry divisions, İsmet commanded two army corps of six infantry divisions, Refet had two infantry divisions and opposing the French at Adana were two more infantry divisions. The III Corps (two infantry divisions) and two independent infantry and two cavalry divisions remained in the interior near Ankara. The weapons which had been hidden from the Allied inspectors began to be recovered and distributed among these armies. Kemal now wielded a powerful instrument, which, in turn, he had given over to trusted and capable subordinate commanders.

In September 1920, Kemal unleashed Karabekir, who rapidly recaptured Sarıkamış from the Armenians at the end of the month. The Turks drove onwards and recaptured Kars on 24–29 October 1920 to re-establish the eastern border. In the south-east the nationalists drove the French and Armenians from Gaziantep and Adana in December. These victories were achieved over weak forces, which had little political backing from the European powers. The first real test of the revived nationalist army came in early 1921, when the long-awaited Greek offensive erupted towards Kütahya and Eskişehir. This came at a bad time because İsmet was preoccupied with crushing the final remnants of the Çerkes Ethem rebellion, which finally ended on 23 January.

Nevertheless, as the Hellenic Army Corps C drove towards Eskişehir, İsmet decided to make a stand on 8 January and positioned the reinforced 24th Infantry Division north of the small town of Inönü. At the same time, the Hellenic Army Corps A attacked toward Afyonkarahisar in Refet's front. Shifting regiments rapidly along the front, İsmet pushed back the Greeks the next day and brought up his 11th Infantry Division on 10/11 January to counter-attack the enemy. He reinforced the battle with the 4th Infantry Division and the 2nd and 3rd Cavalry Divisions and, by 13 January, had pushed the Greeks back 30km. By the end of the month, İsmet had reclaimed almost 100km of territory. Casualties were extremely light and the Turks named this victory the battle of First İnönü.

On 16 March 1921, Kemal's ambassador in Moscow (Ali Fuat Pasha) signed the Turkish-Soviet Treaty of Friendship. This was an important political accomplishment for Kemal because it ended the

Kemal and İnönü. Going back to the 1918 retreat of Kemal's Seventh Army in Syria, İsmet İnönü proved a capable and trustworthy subordinate. Kemal's confidence in his abilities grew over the years. In 1938, Atatürk hand picked İnönü to succeed him as president of the Republic. (Mesut Uyar)

diplomatic isolation of the nationalist government with international recognition of the new Turkish state. Militarily, the treaty contained clauses that solidified the eastern frontier and ended permanently the Armenian threat. Soviet arms shipments, including artillery, machine guns and aircraft, continued to flow to Kemal's army and provided an important component in re-equipping his forces. Counterbalancing this success, the Greeks launched an

Nationalist artillery in the War of Independence. Kemal's artillerymen were mostly regulars with experience in World War I. In this painting nationalist gunners man a German 77mm gun, while an elderly civilian volunteer brings a jug of water to the gun crew. (Atatürk and Independence War Museum)

offensive campaign on 27 March again aimed at Eskişehir and Afyonkarahisar. Cumulatively known as the battle of Second İnönü, the fighting raged through the end of March. İsmet held his position successfully in battles that brought in his 1st, 11th, 24th and 61st Infantry Divisions and the 3rd Cavalry Division. However, in the south, Refet was forced to abandon Afyonkarahisar as the situation there deteriorated rapidly. Kemal responded by reinforcing Refet strongly with infantry, cavalry and artillery. Refet's now powerful and revived Southern Front now contained XII Corps with the 23rd and 57th Infantry Divisions, the independent 4th, 8th, 41st Infantry Divisions, and the 1st and 2nd Cavalry Divisions and he retook the city. At the strategic level, Kemal demonstrated great skill in the allocation of reserves to the Western and Southern Fronts appropriately.

Subsequent battles continued to rage in April in the south as Refet continued his counteroffensive. On 8 April, Refet's XII Corps attacked northwards while the independent divisions, under his personal command, attacked at Aslihanlar. On 11/12 April he tried to outflank the Hellenic 2nd and 13th Infantry Divisions with his cavalry divisions but was stopped by a

Nationalist cavalry in the War of Independence. The cavalry of V Cavalry Corps played a decisive role in the encirclement and destruction of two Greek army corps in 1922. In this painting Turkish cavalry are shown pouring through a break in the Greek lines. (Atatürk and Independence War Museum)

determined counter-attack. Refet fought a further battle at Dumlupınar on 13–15 April to an inconclusive result and, as a consequence, was relieved as the Southern Front commander. On 4 May 1921, İsmet, who was Kemal's most trusted lieutenant, assumed command of both fronts facing the Greeks.

To accommodate more effective command and control, Kemal reorganized İsmet 's force into a well-balanced field army composed of corps-sized groups. By 15 June, the restructured Western Front headquarters commanded I Group (1st, 11th, 23rd and 61st Infantry Divisions and the 3rd Cavalry Division), III Group (4th, 24th and 41st Infantry Divisions and the 1st Cavalry Division), IV Group (5th Caucasian Division, 7th and 8th Infantry Divisions and the 2nd Cavalry Division), and XII Group (57th Infantry Division, a provisional infantry division and the 4th Cavalry Division). Additionally, İsmet commanded the independent 6th and 15th Infantry Divisions, the 3rd Caucasian Division and the 14th Cavalry Division, which he kept under army control.

The Greeks spent the months of May and June reorganizing and repositioning their army in Anatolia. They had made a fundamental error by failing to mass their forces on a single geographic objective. The twin advances towards Eskişehir and Afyonkarahisar were not mutually supporting and led to the Greek defeats. Undeterred by these setbacks, the Greek prime minister and minister of war journeyed to Izmir in late April 1921 for consultations with the commanders of the Field Army of Asia Minor (FAAM). They found that the morale of the Hellenic army was good and that the staff estimated Kemal had about 70,000 men with 200 artillery pieces in the field against their 100,000 men and 238 artillery pieces and they determined to renew the offensive. However, the Hellenic general staff gave up its geographically based strategy and set their campaign objective as the destruction of the Turkish army. They intended to do this by massing their forces and conducting a large-scale decisive engagement. Reinforcements and equipment poured in and the army began to reposition itself for an offensive that was designed to break the back of Turkish resistance.

The Greeks finalized their plan on 4 June 1921, which massed almost the entire field army against İsmet's Western Front. A northern group composed of Army Corps C would attack towards Eskişehir to pin Turkish forces there. Simultaneously the main effort composed of Army Corps A and B, supported by several independent infantry divisions, would swing north to seize Kütahya, thus flanking the Turks. By massing over 100,000 Greeks against 33,000 Turkish infantry and 3,400 cavalry, İsmet's Western Front would be caught between the Greek forces and crushed. In essence, the Greeks pitted almost their entire field forces against less than half of what the Turks had available. Meanwhile, minor operations continued as the Greeks brought their corps into their assembly areas in preparation for the offensive.

Kemal and the national assembly were aware that the Greeks intended to make a maximum effort in Anatolia and had instituted conscription in order to maintain the strength of the army. As a result, Turkish forces in western Anatolia began to near overall manpower parity with the Greeks, though their equipment remained poor. As the Greek offensive approached, their overall forces included 126,000 men, 410 artillery pieces and 4,000 machine guns opposed by 122,000 Turks armed with 160 artillery pieces and 700 machine guns.

On 10 July 1921, the Greeks launched their long-awaited offensive designed to end the war. Kütahya fell on 17 July and the powerful Hellenic army pushed through towards Eskişehir, which fell several days later. Alarmed by the rapidly deteriorating situation, Kemal left Ankara and went to İsmet's headquarters to review and discuss what to do. Kemal ordered İsmet to save the army from destruction and to withdraw step-by-step to a new position east of the Sakarya River. İsmet proposed counter-attacking to reclaim Eskişehir, and, if this failed, he would withdraw as Kemal asked. Kemal agreed and returned to Ankara, and, following an unsuccessful counter-attack on 21 July, İsmet began to pull his army eastwards. To the south, a Turkish cavalry force under Fahrettin was unable to prevent the advance of a supporting Greek attack and Afyonkarahisar was abandoned on 23 July to the Greeks as well. Although he had difficulty communicating this to his subordinates, Kemal understood that, while the nationalists could trade territory for time, they could not withstand the loss of İsmet's field army.

The Hellenic army maintained its momentum and pushed onwards towards Ankara. However, the operational objective of trapping and crushing the Turkish army remained unfulfilled as İsmet conducted a skilful retreat. The Greeks conducted an operational pause to regroup and consider what to do next. On 1 August, they resumed their offensive, this time aiming to seize the nationalist's capital at Ankara. Seven days later, the Greeks were about 50km from Ankara. The nationalist government prepared to evacuate its offices and the families of the ministers and deputies. As the enemy closed in on the capital, an unsteady and nervous national assembly passed a temporary law on 5 August making Kemal the army's commander-in-chief, an authority hitherto reserved exclusively for the Ottoman Sultan, and empowered him to mobilize the economy and population of Anatolia.

Kemal's immediate and draconian actions taken as commander-in-chief form an important part of the contemporary Turkish historical narrative. Famously, Kemal rushed Russian weapons to the embattled front using oxcarts and the labour of peasant women. He requisitioned supplies, including underwear, oxen and carts, and 40 per cent of all leather, cloth, flour and candles for the army. He rehabilitated Refet by appointing him minister of war and charged him with organizing the movement of supplies to the front lines. Deserters, who had become a major drain on the field army, were rounded up and returned to duty. In effect, Kemal ordered the total mobilization of the impoverished Turkish nation and, in response, the people threw their collective will and toil into the war effort. On 17 August 1921, Kemal went to İsmet's headquarters at Polatlı and took personal command of the army in the field.

Kemal established his own headquarters in the small village of Alagöz but was housebound with a broken rib. Accounts cast him as determined

Mustafa Kemal surrounded by Turks before The Great Offensive. The commander-in-chief relaxes with a cigarette while surrounded by representatives of the entire Turkish nation. This painting depicts men and women of all the ethnic groups living in Turkey, including Arabs and Circassians. (Atatürk and Independence War Museum)

but stricken with occasional bouts of despair. The Greeks broke through in several places and Kemal now ordered that every inch of ground be held at all costs. A new defensive line was established and İsmet went to work fortifying it. As the Hellenic army closed on İsmet's positions on the Gök and Sakarya Rivers, the 21-day battle of Sakarya began in earnest on 23 August and lasted until 13 September. The Turkish situation looked bleak but the Hellenic army, led from November 1920 by General Anastasios Papoulas and commanded by King Constantine in person, had reached its culminating point – although that was yet to be recognized.

Greek infantry attacked across the entire line and penetrated in some places. The decisive moment came on 2 September when, after bitter hand-to-hand combat, the Greeks seized a key hill top named Çaldag (Mount Chal). The exhausted Greeks had reached the high water mark of their campaign to wrest Asia Minor from the Turks. With the situation stabilized, Kemal came forward on 8 September and personally led a counter-attack which took the hill back. İsmet then launched vigorous counter-attacks that pushed the Greeks back all along the front. Finally, Papoulas called off the offensive and began to disengage with a view to occupying positions to the west of the river. Casualties were about even with the Turks losing 3,700 killed and 18,000 wounded and the Greeks losing 4,000 killed and 19,000 wounded. However, the retreating Greeks were forced to abandon many of the wounded as they pulled back (perhaps as many as 15,000). Kemal called Sakarya an 'officer's battle' as the army lost 300 officers killed and 1,000 wounded out of a total of 5,000 present. Kemal returned to Ankara on 18 September and delivered an inspiring victory speech to the assembly.

However, Papoulas was not yet defeated mentally and was determined to regain the initiative. From crisis there is sometimes opportunity and, with the bulk of the Turkish army drawn to the Sakarya battlefield, Papoulas sensed Turkish vulnerability elsewhere. He shifted Army Corps B south and launched an offensive against Afyonkarahisar on 29 September. After a week-long battle the city fell to the Greeks and Army Corps B pushed more than 20km to the east. Thus, as October arrived, the Greeks held a line that began at Iznik (ancient Nicaea) bulging east to Eskişehir and then running south to Afyonkarahisar before running back to the west near Uşak. This created a strategic salient deep into Turkish territory, but at the same time created a bulge that could be easily attacked by the Turks. According to the official Hellenic army history, 'Thus ended the campaign to capture Ankara'. The Greeks refused to believe that they had been beaten on the battlefield preferring to attribute defeat to the lack of reserves and supplies. The Turks, on the other hand, attributed victory to the steady hand and presence on the battlefield of their commander-in-chief.

On 14 October 1921, Kemal revised the command architecture of the Western Front once again by forming the First Army under the command of Ali İhsan (Sabis) as well

Women in the War of Independence. An iconic image in the modern Turkish historical narrative is the role of women and the elderly in the war of Independence. In this painting Turkish women load shells into an ox cart while others reload bullets on the workbench behind. (Atatürk and Independence War Museum)

as redesignating most of the groups into numbered army corps. Unusually for the Turks, who had dissolved their last cavalry corps in 1914, V Group was converted into V Cavalry Corps, concentrating the 2nd, 3rd and 14th Cavalry Divisions under a single tactical commander. İsmet retained command over the new army as well as over the Kocaeli Group in the north. On 1 December, the Second Army was activated under the command of Yakub Şevki (Subaşı) and assigned to İsmet's control as well. At this time, the First Army retained command of I and IV Corps, V Cavalry Corps and the independent 6th Infantry Division, while the new Second Army was assigned II Corps, the 8th, 16th and 17th Infantry Divisions and the 1st Cavalry Division. Kemal was building an army group capable of conducting offensive operations at the operational level of war. Importantly, this effort was partially enabled by the signing of two diplomatic agreements. The first with France on 20 October, under which they evacuated Cilicia and secured the Syrian border and the second, the Kars Pact on 22 October 1921 with the Soviets, which secured the Caucasian frontier. These agreements, by stabilizing the eastern and southern borders, had the strategic effect of allowing Kemal to concentrate men and resources against the Greeks. In the meantime, there were minor battles over the course of the winter and spring of 1922, but overall the Greek front remained stable.

Throughout the winter, Refet worked relentlessly to improve the lines of communications in order to reconstitute the field army's logistical posture. Damaged rail lines were repaired and motor transportation consolidated and moved to centralized locations. Artillery ammunition was acquired and safely stored for future use. Medical care and nutrition for men and animals alike were improved. Under Kemal's guidance, training centres and military courses were created for specialists and soldiers. By January 1922, the Western Front had 72,000 rifles, 538 light and 582 heavy machine guns on hand. Moreover, İsmet's artillery strength had grown to 324 artillery pieces as well. In February, a system of bread-baking companies was created in the corps rear areas and in March the major headquarters were connected by telephone lines. In

Turkish nationalist pilots during the War of Independence. Most of the nationalist aircraft were procured from the French (a Breuget bomber is shown here), although there were some German aircraft, which were left behind during at the end of World War I. (Stuart Kline)

April and May, the reliable and consistent flow of food and ammunition to the front-line units became a reality. As the weather grew more temperate, the army began a series of field training manoeuvres and command exercises. Kemal was creating the training and logistical base necessary to support large-scale combat operations at the operational level of war. However, while supplies and ammunition remained at a threshold sufficient for defensive purposes, they stubbornly remained at levels that were insufficient to support a major attack, and plans for a spring offensive were delayed.

On the other side of the line, the overextended Hellenic army likewise had difficulty supplying its forces so far from the Aegean port of Izmir and also experienced shortages of all kinds. As a result they grew steadily weaker and, in May, a discouraged General Papoulas resigned. General Georgios Polymenakos replaced him. As summer approached, repeated attempts by the western powers and by the Greek government to secure some kind of armistice, which retained a portion of Turkish Anatolia, failed and the political will in Athens necessary to sustain the war began to fail as well. While the Turks were growing stronger politically and militarily, the Greeks, in turn, were growing relatively weaker. Making things worse operationally, the Greek high command maintained a dangerous concentration of strength, their Army Corps A and B, in the Afyonkarahisar bulge, while thinning the lines to the north and south of the city. In addition to this, in June the Hellenic Army Corps D launched an occupation of eastern Thrace that drew substantial Greek strength to the gates of Istanbul, further diluting Greek forces in Anatolia.

First Army, 24 August 1922

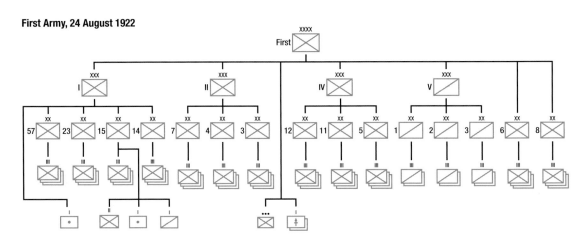

Second Army, 24 August 1922

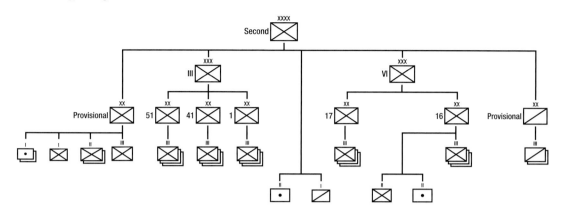

Recognizing the Greeks' vulnerability and preoccupation with Istanbul, on 16 June 1922, Kemal instructed Fevzi, his chief of staff, to start preparing an offensive planning directive, which was completed and sent to İsmet two weeks later. On 3 July, İsmet sent Kemal the outlines of his operational plan, which named the First Army as the main effort with I Corps, IV Corps and V Cavalry Corps sweeping behind Afyonkarahisar from the south, while the Second Army's supporting attack by VI Corps pushed in from the north. II Corps was to be shifted from the Second Army to First Army as the reserve for the main effort. Second Army's III Corps main task was to conduct a supporting effort to tie down a response by the Hellenic Army Corps C. If properly and rapidly executed, the plan aimed at encircling the Hellenic Army Corps A and B. Kemal approved the plan on the following day, with minor adjustments to the strength of II Corps. İsmet began to brief his subordinates on 4 July, one of whom was the newly assigned Nurettin ('Sakallı', Konyar), who replaced Ali İhsan as First Army Commander. Nurettin was an extremely aggressive field commander and had conducted the pursuit and encirclement of British Major-General Charles Townshend's army from Ctesiphon to Kut al-Amara in Iraq in November 1915. He was an ideal choice to execute the mission assigned to the First Army.

The mature plan reflected the classic hallmarks of Kemal and İsmet's German-style military education from their days as young officers in the Ottoman War Academy. The plan employed economy of force (Second Army in the role of 'anvil') while massing the bulk of the available combat

The American four-stack destroyer, USS Litchfield, just offshore during the burning of Smyrna in September 1922. Allied warships, including British battleships, French and Italian cruisers and four American destroyers, assisted in the evacuation of thousands of Greeks and other Europeans as the city burned to the ground. (Library of Congress)

strength in the main effort (First Army in the role of 'hammer'). The highly mobile cavalry corps would be used to encircle the Greeks and finish them off in a Cannae-like battle of annihilation. As word of the impending offensive spread, morale in the Turkish army soared. As finally matched, the Turks had 199,000 men including 100,000 infantry, 2,025 light and 839 heavy machine guns, and 323 artillery pieces. To oppose this force, the Greeks had 218,000 men including 90,000 infantry, 3,139 light and 1,280 heavy machine guns, and 418 artillery pieces. Although the forces were fairly balanced numerically, the Turks enjoyed a material superiority in

The Great Offensive, 26 August 1922

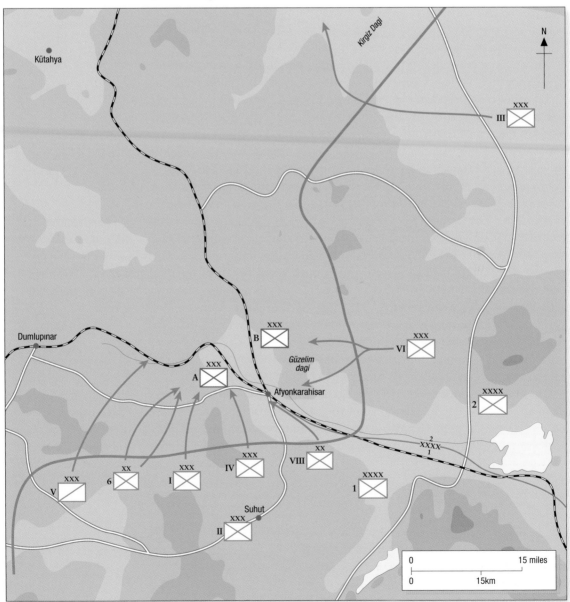

cavalry of 5,282 swords to the Greeks' 1,280. Only in aircraft did the Greeks maintain superiority with 50 machines to the Turks' ten.

In the first weeks of August, İsmet's divisions moved forwards to their assembly positions. Major unit movements brought II Corps into Nurettin's sector and shifted V Cavalry Corps to the far left flank of his First Army. Kemal left Ankara and established his headquarters at Akşehir on 20 August. To maintain secrecy, his staff kept up his social calendar, including a 21 August tea party in Ankara. On 25 August, Kemal joined the First Army's battle headquarters and all communications with Ankara were cut off. The battle began on 26 August 1922 with a brief artillery preparation on the Greek lines fired at 5am, after which the Turkish infantry attacked. Kemal, İsmet, Fevzi and Nurettin gathered at Kocatepe Hill at dawn to observe the launching of what the Turks would come to call 'The Great Offensive' (*Büyük Taarruz*). The Turkish artillery barrages were particularly devastating, which reflected the effectiveness of Kemal's emphasis on training and planning. Nevertheless, the entrenched Greeks resisted strongly and, by the end of the day, the Turks had made progress but had not achieved a breakthrough.

The critical moment came at 7am the next morning, when the Turkish IV Corps seized the Erikmen heights, opening the Greek line to destruction. This was followed at noon by I Corps breaking the line in its sector as well. In the meantime, Fahrettin's V Cavalry Corps readied itself for action and pushed north that evening, while the reserve II Corps moved forwards as well. The Turks were poised to execute their planned encirclement of the Greeks.

At 4.30am, 27 August 1922, İsmet ordered V Cavalry Corps to conduct a reconnaissance towards Dumlupınar and, at 3.30pm, he ordered the corps into an exploitation in the enemy's rear. At the same time, he ordered his I and IV Corps to conduct a pursuit of the fleeing Greeks. Afyonkarahisar fell that afternoon and the Hellenic Army Corps A and B began a precipitous retreat to the west in order to extricate themselves from the trap. The First Army continued its northward push throughout the night of 27/28 August. Kemal arrived that evening in Afyonkarahisar and shared deliberations with İsmet. Just after midnight, İsmet issued orders directing the First Army to shift westwards to encircle the retreating Greeks.

The next morning the Turks were in full pursuit of the collapsing Hellenic army and V Cavalry Corps thrust north to cut off the enemy retreat routes. As the trap closed, II Corps was brought forward in case it was needed. From the north, the Second Army pushed its cavalry divisions south throughout the day. The day ended with the breakup of Greek command and control as the beaten Hellenic Army Corps A and B tried to funnel out to safety through Dumlupınar. The Hellenic army's official history of the campaign uses the word 'fragments' to describe the condition of the army. The Greek corps commanders, Major-General Charilaos Trikoupes of Army Corps A and Major-General Kimon Digenes of Army Corps B, merged their headquarters in an attempt to bring some cohesion to their operations. Trikoupes was the senior of the two and assumed overall tactical direction of the retreat. On 29 August, the Turks compressed the remaining Greek

Kemal after the war of Independence. Kazım Karabekır stands to Kemal's right and his wife, Latifa, stands just behind him. (Mesut Uyar)

forces into a small perimeter and İsmet ordered V Cavalry Corps to turn back and link up with I Corps in order to seal the escape route completely.

Impatient as always, and concerned that İsmet's armies were not moving fast enough to trap the Greek formations, Kemal went forward himself to direct operations on the morning of 30 August. He went to IV Corps headquarters and sent Fevzi up to the Second Army headquarters to push them forward as well. Caught in the Turkish pincers was an ad hoc collection of units known as the 'Trikoupes Group', which was composed of the surviving remnants of five infantry divisions and miscellaneous corps troops. Kemal moved his command post to a low hill now called Zafertepe (Victory Hill) but soon found that the situation was so confused that it was almost impossible to improve on what İsmet's commanders were already accomplishing. The Hellenic FAAM disintegrated and the survivors of five divisions (4th, 5th, 9th, 12th, and 13th Infantry Divisions) surrendered in packets as the day progressed. Trikoupes, his command group – including Major-General Digenes – and about 6,000 men managed to infiltrate out of the trap by hiking over the mountains to the north-west. The Turks commemorate Kemal's personal participation in this battle by calling it the battle of the Commander-in-Chief (*Baskumandan Meydan Muharebesi*).

On 31 August, Kemal met with Fevzi and İsmet to discuss the strategic situation. Fevzi proposed dividing the effort by sending the Second Army north towards Izmit and the First Army onward towards Izmir. İsmet argued that both armies should pursue the main enemy to Izmir without giving them time to re-establish a defensive line. He reasoned that his army had exhausted their ammunition and although it could not fight a second major battle in the near future it still retained the ability to march rapidly and concentrate. Kemal agreed with İsmet and ordered a pursuit (a pursuit is a doctrinal term to describe a military operation in which a defeated enemy force is literally chased to destruction). He ordered the armies forward on 1 September towards Izmir and concluded his orders dramatically with 'Armies! The Mediterranean is your immediate objective. Forward!'

The next day, the Turks reorganized themselves and launched a vigorous pursuit of the retreating Greeks, whose Army Corps A and B had been shattered and literally destroyed as fighting formations. On the night of 2/3 September, V Cavalry Corps caught up with and surrounded the Trikoupes Group near Uşak and forced its surrender. Both Hellenic army corps commanders, hundreds of machine guns, a dozen artillery pieces, 500 officers and another 5,000 men went into the Turkish prisoner of war camps. Over the following week, the First Army's I and IV Corps marched nonstop towards Izmir, while V Cavalry Corps continuously harried and outflanked the Greeks on the army's right flank. It was a classically executed pursuit operation matching Napoleon's 1806 Jena–Auerstadt campaign. On 9 September 1922, Kemal's cavalry liberated the city of Izmir. Unfortunately, most of the city subsequently burned to the ground in circumstances that remain suspicious to this day. The relentless pursuit did not stop and the remaining Hellenic army units were pushed to the small port of Kuşadası, where their navy evacuated them. Another smaller wing of Kemal's army pushed north simultaneously liberating the Koceli peninsula and the shore of the Sea of Marmara. The Great Idea and the Greeks were finished in Asia Minor.

Mustafa Kemal after the War of Independence. This portrait of a mature general is a common sight in modern Turkey and appears in many private businesses and public office spaces. (Mesut Uyar)

The cost of the three-year war to the new Turkish nation was substantial – 13,000 officers and men killed and 35,000 wounded. In the final campaign Kemal's armies lost 13,000 killed, wounded and missing. The war punished Greece, which had a population a third the size of Turkey's, even more – the final campaign cost them 70,000 men, of whom 35,000 were prisoners of war, while half of their army's equipment and weapons was lost in the disastrous retreat from Afyonkarahisar.

Kemal was not finished yet, however, as the British still held Istanbul while the Greeks occupied eastern Thrace. He sent his armies north and, on 23 September, Turkish cavalry entered the straits neutral zone. Five days later, the 2nd Cavalry Division closed on the British positions at the Dardanelles. Turkish soldiers now stood nose-to-nose with British soldiers and historians know this as the Chanak Crisis. The Allies, exhausted and financially weak from World War I, were alarmed by the aggressive nationalists but were determined to resolve the crisis diplomatically. Notes were exchanged between the British, the French and the Turks and they agreed to begin armistice negotiations on 3 October at Mudanya, which was the port of the city of Bursa on the Sea of Marmara. Kemal appointed İsmet as his representative and gave him explicit instructions not to give up anything in the talks. Circumstances favoured the Turks; the Allies were war weary, an anti-war coup had just overthrown the Greek government, and the nationalists possessed the initiative. The negotiations lasted a week and İsmet proved to be tough-minded and focused. The Turks and the Allies signed the armistice agreement on 10 October 1922, but the Greeks did not. The agreement returned Istanbul, Edirne and the Dardanelles to the Turks and expelled the Hellenic army from eastern Thrace. The next day, III Corps pushed to the Asian suburbs of Istanbul and 6,000 infantrymen and 1,000 cavalrymen from the army were appointed as gendarmes under Refet's command and deployed into the reclaimed territory.

In late October, the Allies invited the Turks to a peace conference at Lausanne, Switzerland, which would formally end World War I in the Middle East. The Allies had belatedly recognized that the unfair conditions imposed on the Turks by the Sèvres Treaty were fundamentally untenable. Unsurprisingly, Kemal again sent İsmet as the new nation's negotiator to the conference, which convened on 21 November 1922. Earlier agreements had already defined most of Turkey's borders but the possession of Mosul in Iraq became the most contentious issue. In the end, İsmet lost Mosul but secured economic concessions in return. The conference dragged on for months but was finally signed on 24 July 1923. İsmet returned to Ankara on 13 August, which was also the same day that the Second Grand National Assembly elected Kemal as its president. One part of the treaty that had immediate consequences for many was the compulsory exchanges of populations. Within the year, over a million ethnic Greeks from Anatolia and Thrace were involuntarily relocated to Greece. Reciprocally, 380,000 Muslims were forcibly relocated from Greece to Turkey. While some individuals and small communities remained behind, this act amounted to what is, today, termed ethnic cleansing. Of note, the Patriarchy of the Greek Orthodox Church remained in its historic home in Istanbul.

Kemal triumphant

Field Marshal and Commander-in-Chief Mustafa Kemal overlooking his army during the Turkish War of Independence. Kemal (1) and his principal commanders – İsmet (2), Fevzi (3) and Nurettin (4), gathered on Kocatepe Hill to observe the opening barrage at 5am on 26 August 1922 as the Great Offensive began. Carefully trained and magnificently led, Kemal's Nationalist Army became the instrument of victory and liberation. Kemal envisioned the Great Offensive as a classic encirclement campaign of annihilation in the German tradition. Within three days, the Turks broke through the shattered Hellenic Army nearly encircling the enemy. As was his habit, Kemal went forward to command the final push which, on 30 August, saw the encirclement and surrender of five Greek infantry divisions. Kemal's inspired leadership is commemorated in Turkey today by calling this part of the campaign the 'Battle of the Commander-in-Chief'.

Kemal ordered his armies into a vigorous pursuit of the disintegrating Hellenic Army with his famous command, 'Armies! The Mediterranean is your immediate objective. Forward!' Several days later, Kemal's soldiers forced the surrender of 5,000 more Greeks including two army corps commanders. Relentlessly pursuing the enemy, the Turks swept down out of the hills of Anatolia reaching and capturing Izmir (then known as Smyrna) on the Mediterranean Sea on 9 September 1922. Altogether, the Greeks lost over 70,000 men in this campaign as well as half of their army's equipment. This victorious campaign consolidated the Nationalist position and set the conditions for the establishment of the modern Turkish Republic.

Mustafa Kemal emerged from this campaign as a proven operational commander and strategic leader of great ability. Moreover, he demonstrated that he was an organizer and trainer with an unusual capacity to create a modern army with a powerful offensive capability as well as high morale.

Mustafa Kemal as military commander

The long series of wars that defined the first half of Mustafa Kemal's life were over. Starting as a military academy cadet he reached the pinnacle of command as his nation's commander-in-chief in a remarkably short time. But it must be highlighted that what was a short span in a chronological career included an unusually large amount of time spent in combat. Moreover, Kemal's climb to the top is all the more astonishing when considering the extreme variety of climates, terrain and operations in which he fought.

Lieutenant-General William Birdwood, Commander of the Australian-New Zealand Army Corps at Gallipoli. Birdwood went on to a very successful tour as an army commander in the BEF in France. He retired in 1930 and was raised to Baron Birdwood of Anzac in 1938. That same year he represented the king at Mustafa Kemal's funeral. (AWM, G00761)

As a junior officer, Kemal commanded soldiers engaged in counter-insurgency operations in the Negev Desert and in the mountains of Macedonia, as well as serving on the staff of a field army headquarters. He spent a year in the deserts and hills of Libya organizing and leading guerrillas against the Italians. An assignment as an army chief of operations and chief of staff fighting the Bulgarians on the Gallipoli peninsula in deliberate defensive, hasty offensive and pursuit operations rounded out his professional experiences. As a division commander fighting the Australians, he conducted a successful meeting engagement and hasty defence. Subsequently, he commanded corps-sized hasty attacks in the rugged terrain of Gallipoli. At Anafarta, Kemal commanded a corps-level combat group conducting defensive operations and counter-attacks. He led his corps in deliberate offensive operations against the Russians in the Caucasus Mountains. As an army commander in the dry semi-deserts of Palestine, he conducted one of the most skilful retreats of the 20th century under relentless British pressure. In his capacity as commander-in-chief, he commanded at army group level in western Anatolia against the Greeks. Kemal orchestrated the reconstitution and retraining of the nationalist forces after which he planned the magnificent operational encirclement of two Greek army corps and personally led the final closing of the encircling pincers. This was followed by a strategic pursuit which ended in the expulsion of the Greeks from Asia Minor.

He was generally successful everywhere and often spectacularly so. All of these experiences were crammed into a 17-year period and it must be considered that, most of the time, he led a multi-ethnic, non-industrialized, largely illiterate army of conscripted peasants. Arguably his greatest accomplishments were his defensive operations at Gallipoli, his retreat in Palestine and Syria, and his revival of the nationalist army leading to the defeat of the Greeks in 1922. It is hard to imagine an alternative history in which the Ottomans and the Turkish nationalists might have done better without the presence of Mustafa Kemal.

OPPOSING COMMANDERS

There is some difficulty in the selection of precisely who the opposing commanders might be position for position. For example, on 25 April 1915, as the Gallipoli battle escalated Kemal sequentially fought Colonel Ewen Sinclair-MacLagan, Major-General W. T. Bridges and Lieutenant-General Sir William Birdwood. In Palestine, he often fought the cavalry of the Desert Mounted Corps commanded by Major-General Henry Chauvel, but a case can be made that in the final stages of the campaign Kemal opposed General Sir Edmund Allenby himself. As president and commander-in-chief, his actual counterpart was King Constantine of Greece, although his opponent on the ground was General Georgios Polymenakos and, in the end, Major-General Charilaos Trikoupes. This section will, therefore, focus on the commanders Kemal opposed at Gallipoli in 1915, in Palestine in 1918 and in western Anatolia in 1922.

Gallipoli

Kemal's principal opponent throughout the Gallipoli campaign was Lieutenant-General Sir William Birdwood, the commander of the Australian and New Zealand Army Corps. Birdwood was born in India in 1865 and educated in England at Clifton College, Bristol. He was commissioned in the infantry out of Sandhurst but transferred to the Indian Army cavalry, serving in the Bengal Lancers and 12th Lancers from 1885 to 1899. He served on the North-West Frontier in regimental and staff assignments and rose rapidly to the rank of colonel (1905). Birdwood was a sportsman and great horseman. He was fortunate to serve in the Boer War with the Natal Mounted Brigade where he proved to be a brave and capable troop leader. After being wounded he was assigned to Lord Herbert Kitchener's personal staff and became his protégé.

Subsequently in India, Birdwood's association with Kitchener gained him early promotions to high rank and in 1914 he was a major-general of three years' standing. He never attended the staff colleges and never earned the prestigious 'p.s.c.' (passed staff college), which marked so many of his contemporaries in World War I. Oddly, he was often remembered for his passion for gardening and reading newspapers rather than for any interest in military affairs. When the war began Kitchener was appointed as Secretary of State for War and remembered Birdwood, who was then serving in Delhi, India. In late November 1914, Kitchener asked Birdwood to take command of the ANZAC then en route to Egypt from Australia. His principal biographer characterized him as 'not outstanding as a tactician, nor had he the cast of mind peculiar to an organizer'. That said, in overall terms, Birdwood was a fortunate selection to command the ANZAC because his real strength as a commander was his leadership style, which pivoted on a likable personality and warmth toward soldiers. These qualities, plus his extreme personal bravery, immediately endeared him to the Australians. Beyond this, if Birdwood had a skill, it was in his uncanny ability to surround himself with excellent subordinates.

General Sir Edmund Allenby. Nicknamed 'the Bull', Allenby was forceful and headstrong. He was victorious against the Ottomans primarily because of his skills as a trainer of soldiers, mastery of contemporary tactics and his genius as an organizer. He was promoted to field marshal and raised to peerage as Viscount Allenby of Megiddo in 1919. (IWM, Q 82969)

Birdwood was delighted when an old friend and former commander General Sir Ian Hamilton was appointed to command the Mediterranean Expeditionary Force (MEF) in early 1915. Birdwood's ANZAC was assigned to the MEF and tasked with making a supporting assault at Gallipoli on 25 April. In Egypt, throughout its preparation for this offensive, the ANZAC focused on individual and small unit training at the expense of combined arms and division-level exercises. On the morning of 25 April, the ANZAC landings went badly awry and were followed by more errors in the placement of the ANZAC main body as it came ashore. Birdwood's personal focus that day was on getting his corps off the ships and onto the shore, which he managed to do very successfully. However, by mid-afternoon, even though Birdwood had 15,000 men on shore opposed by Kemal's 5,000, both corps- and division-level command and control had broken down entirely. At the end of the day, the ANZAC failed to takes its objective and there were too many troops in some places and too few in others. Conspicuously absent from the ANZAC lodgement were enough artillery pieces to counter the intense Ottoman artillery fire. Some historians believe that Gallipoli was a systemic failure in British command systems rather than in the personal failures of individual commanders and there is much truth in this idea. By midnight, Birdwood had failed notably to demonstrate adequate situational awareness of the operational and tactical environment. Faced with what he felt were stark choices, Birdwood abrogated his responsibility and asked his friend Ian Hamilton to evacuate the ANZAC.

In the following defensive battles over the summer, however, Birdwood demonstrated growth as a commander and proved to be an inspirational combat leader. In the summer of 1915, it was Birdwood and his staff who came up with the idea of a wide flanking movement to break the deadlock on the peninsula. In early August, the ANZAC, with X Corps landing at Suvla Bay to guard its flank, launched an offensive on Chunuk Bair. Birdwood chose surprise over preparation and rehearsals, and the consequences of this decision doomed the attack to fail. Although Birdwood subsequently became an effective corps and army commander on the Western Front under General Sir Douglas Haig, it is arguable that he was always a step behind Kemal and the Ottomans at Gallipoli.

Palestine

The British army in Palestine that opposed Kemal in 1918 was a greatly different army to the one he had fought previously at Gallipoli. Notably, it was a tactically skilled, well-trained and well-organized force and these strengths came directly from the assignment of General Sir Edmund Allenby in the summer of 1917. Allenby's reorganization of the ad hoc Egyptian Expeditionary Force (EEF) to mirror the British Expeditionary Force (BEF) in France enabled the introduction of modern artillery and infantry tactics.

This resulted in the twin victories of Beersheba and Third Gaza. Allenby's subsequent retraining of a largely Indian force in the summer of 1918 then created an army that was far advanced tactically compared with its Ottoman opponent.

Allenby was born in Nottinghamshire in 1861 and joined the cavalry after Sandhurst. Like Birdwood, he learned soldiering on the empire's frontiers – but in Africa rather than India. Unlike Birdwood, he chose to attend the staff college at Camberley, earning the distinctive 'p.s.c.', but was not known as

a military intellectual. Allenby commanded well in the Boer War and rose to become a major-general in 1909. He was the Inspector of Cavalry and went to France in August 1914 as the commander of the BEF's Cavalry Division. He rose to command a corps on the Western Front but fell out with Haig in 1917 and was sent to Egypt. Assigned to command the EEF, Allenby's experience and education came to the fore and he proved to be a master organizer and peerless trainer of men. He reorganized the force to leverage his immense artillery superiority and created, at long last, an effective combined arms British ground force in the Middle East. In short order, his army pushed the Ottomans away from the Egyptian frontier and captured Jerusalem.

General Sir Henry George Chauvel. Nicknamed 'Harry', he was the first Australian to be promoted to lieutenant-general and to command an army corps. Later he made full general. Chauvel retired in 1930 but returned to duty in World War II to command the Volunteer Defence Corps (Australia's Home Guard). (AWM, B00326)

The EEF's campaign plan for Megiddo in September 1918 was a model of its kind and explicitly set the annihilation of Liman von Sanders' army as its operational objective. Allenby's deception plan was elaborate as was his use of tactical airpower and, moreover, his tactics mirrored those then being successfully employed at Amiens (although without tanks) in France against the Germans. In addition to his organizational and operational genius, Allenby possessed a natural instinct for mobility from his cavalry background. In his 1917 reorganization of the EEF he activated a cavalry corps and gave its command to an Australian cavalryman named Major-General Henry Chauvel. Chauvel had served in the Boer War in Sir John French's cavalry division and, after the war, spent time in Australia training light horse regiments. He commanded a dismounted light horse brigade at Gallipoli and did well in trench warfare conditions. In Palestine, Chauvel first served as a mounted division commander in the half-cavalry and half-infantry Desert Column. Elevated to command the Desert Mounted Corps, Chauvel played a key role in the envelopment and seizure of Beersheba.

Chauvel showed particular skill in the secret massing of his cavalry corps in the battle of Megiddo. Also of note was his personal coordination with the commanding general of XX Corps, through which his troopers had to ride once the breakthrough of the Ottoman lines was accomplished. This operation is known as a forward passage of lines and is extremely difficult to execute. Chauvel's success in accomplishing this was based on excellent staff work and close coordination with the infantry divisions to establish lanes through which his regiments might pass. In the exploitation north from the Megiddo breakthrough, Allenby gave Chauvel free rein and relied on his initiative and natural aggressiveness to pursue the Ottoman army to destruction. It was Chauvel's cavalry which almost captured Liman von Sanders at Nablus and crossed the Jordan River thus forcing Kemal's Seventh Army to retreat east rather than north. Although Chauvel was not a staff college graduate, he performed very well over the course of the war and in ever-increasing positions of responsibility.

Asia Minor

In 1922, The Hellenic army was a well-established and well-equipped force with a solid reputation. Its commanders and most of its men had combat experience in the Balkan Wars and World War I. However, on the debit side it was operating in enemy country as an overseas expeditionary force and, in the summer of 1922, its logistical lines were stretched to the limit. The Hellenic army reflected Allied military thinking, and was particularly French-like in its thinking, training and tactical doctrines. From 1920 through to 22 May 1922, Lieutenant-General Anastasios Papoulas commanded the FAAM and he was characterized as not having a particularly strong character. After Sakarya, the Hellenic high command experienced a strategic dilemma of whether to stand fast on the defensive or advance on the enemy. Papoulas advocated an advance but was overruled and given an unclear mission which failed to differentiate whether he was supposed to destroy the enemy army or whether he was supposed to take Ankara. In the end Papoulas did neither.

Reviewing troops with İnönü in the 1920s. The soldiers Kemal is inspecting are Turkish storm troopers, who were trained and equipped along the German *Stosstruppen* model. (Mesut Uyar)

This absence of strategic and operational clarity resulted in a broad frontal advance by the Greeks rather than a narrow advance focused on decisive objectives. Papoulas resigned in disgust and was replaced by Lieutenant-General Georgios Chatzanestes (sometimes referred to in the English language literatures as 'Hatzianestis'), who had commanded the Hellenic army in Thrace. Chatzanestes was a trained general staff officer and had been educated in Germany. He moved his headquarters to Izmir in June 1922 and immediately undertook a two-week inspection of the front. He estimated that the army's morale was good but that it was overextended. He thought that the army ought to be withdrawn to shorter and less vulnerable lines. However, his opinion of Kemal's army was low and, consequently, he moved regiments from Asia Minor to Thrace. This was a terrible error which further diluted and weakened Greece's main effort.

Chatzanestes returned to Izmir, where he remained personally out of contact with the situation at the front. The FAAM's 12 divisions were spread thinly along the front with nine infantry divisions concentrated in the three army corps confronting the Turks along the Eskişehir –Afyonkarahisar line. Unfortunately for Greece, Chatzanestes remained personally focused on the capture of Istanbul and was not particularly engaged in supervising the Anatolian front. However, he was experienced enough to recognize his own inability to command effectively in what amounted to two separate theatres. Therefore, Chatzanestes issued orders to the commanders of Army Corps A and B that, in the event of a Turkish attack, Trikoupes would assume command of both corps. When Kemal's Great Offensive struck the Greeks, Chatzanestes found himself surprised and unable to shift forces effectively against the Turks or to adequately organize a retreat. All he managed to do was to place Army Corps B under the command of Army Corps A (Trikoupes) and hope for the best.

For his part, when the Turks attacked, Trikoupes' communications to Izmir were broken and he found himself and his army isolated. Moreover, communications with his front-line infantry divisions also broke down rapidly leaving him unable to issue orders in a timely manner. It is ironic that, with his front collapsing, Trikoupes never received Chatzanestes' bizarre 27 August order to recapture all of the lost positions. Trikoupis attempted to form a cohesive fighting withdrawal but always seemed to be cut off by Turkish cavalry at key locations. The Hellenic government relieved Chatzanestes as commander in Asia Minor and replaced him with Trikoupes on 4 September. It is said that Trikoupes learned of his promotion from Kemal after being captured by the Turks. Later, in November, Chatzanestes and five other leaders were held responsible for the catastrophe and executed by firing squad by the new Hellenic government. At the strategic level, the Greek disaster boiled down to a lack of strategic clarity and a failure to articulate coherent objectives. At the operational level, failure was the outcome of a small army trying to occupy and hold too much ground and, at the tactical level, failure was predetermined by ineffective command and control.

INSIDE THE MIND

There is no question that Mustafa Kemal Atatürk was a complex personality who was, in many ways, a reflection of the changing world in which he lived. His origins in the European provinces of the Ottoman Empire were important determinants in forming his thinking, but it was his association with the Ottoman army that certainly had the most influence intellectually and emotionally on how Atatürk thought.

Reviewing troops in the 1930s. Although the uniforms of the Turkish officers and soldiers are more modern, these are the sons of the men who manned the Ottoman army. The Turks are proud of their military heritage and having an ancestor who fought at Gallipoli remains a point of pride in Turkey to this day. (Mesut Uyar)

After 1826, when the reactionary and tradition-bound Janissaries were eliminated as a force in Ottoman politics, the Ottoman army became the engine of modernity in the empire. In the 19th century, the Ottoman army created a modern educational system for its school-trained officers (*mektepli*), which stressed engineering, languages and western military practices. Most of the Ottoman Sultans encouraged modernization and westernization as well by employing European specialists and importing military technology into the Ottoman Empire. It is no surprise that almost all of the Young Turks had military backgrounds. The three-year curriculum of the Ottoman War Academy especially inculcated its graduates with European ideas, who were trained to practice predominately German military doctrines. War Academy graduates were the elite of the army and this gave them confidence and a sense of certainty about their future prospects and chances of success. As a boy, Kemal was notable for his certitude and focused work ethic but it was the army that harnessed the raw human material to the discipline and mission-oriented thinking of the military.

Professionally, Kemal was intensely ambitious. He worked continuously to achieve high command and he was persistent, especially in the pursuit of his own goals. When he was marginalized in what might have been 'dead-end' jobs he managed to fight his way back into the institutional arena. He was intellectually and physically tough. On a personal level, Kemal was prickly. He could not resist commenting on the work or aspirations of his fellows. He was quick to criticize his superiors and the institutions that he was a part of. This reflected his certitude regarding his own ideas and demonstrated a fundamental courage in the correctness of his own convictions. This trait complemented Kemal's genuine physical courage and this combination made him a dynamic and effective combat commander. However, his tendency towards criticism also hurt him badly and he could never quite seem to exercise the restraint necessary to move seamlessly upward.

After the end of World War I, Kemal demonstrated a penchant for selecting trusted subordinates, who had previously served him well and placing them in key leadership positions. The army, corps and divisional commanders in the nationalist army he created in 1921–22 were almost entirely men who had served with him on the Gallipoli peninsula in 1915. He was loyal to his subordinates up to the point where they criticized him or became a direct political threat to his own aspirations. His most famous protégé was İsmet İnönü, whom was selected to succeed him as president of the Republic before Kemal's 1938.

In his personal life, Kemal enjoyed the company of a number of beautiful and accomplished women, who were also advocates of westernization and supporters of European-style women's rights. After the Balkan wars, Kemal spent a great deal of time in the cultured salon of a young army widow named Corinne in a relationship characterized as an *amitié amoureuse*. It was during this time in Istanbul where he met the beautiful and westernized 16-year-old Fikriye, with whom he maintained an intimate relationship for the next 12 years. She played the piano, was an excellent conversationalist and was devoted to Kemal. Had his mother and sister not objected to Fikriye's suitability, she might have become his wife.

After the great victories of 1922, Kemal met 24-year-old Lâtife in Izmir. She was attractive, had studied law in France and was also very accomplished socially and intellectually. He married her in 1923 in a brief civil ceremony and, for a while, she was very supportive of Kemal's roles as the political leader of Turkey. However, when Kemal continued his alcohol-fuelled late night activities and kept her shut in at home, Lâtife became increasingly frustrated and depressed. When it became evident that Kemal sought the company of male friends for companionship and other women for enjoyment and that he would not change his behaviour, the marriage collapsed. The couple divorced after only two years. Kemal would later claim that he was married to the nation to explain the divorce. Of note, at different points in his life, Kemal adopted a number of children, including the famous Turkish aviatrix, Sabiha Gökçen.

The president of the Republic teaches the alphabet. In this iconic photo, Mustafa Kemal is shown explaining the newly mandated Latinized alphabet to a class of Turks. The law changing Ottoman script to a European-based alphabet has effectively cut off the Turkish people, except for a handful of scholars, from their own history. (Atatürk Research Center)

WHEN WAR IS DONE

The Grand National Assembly established the Republic of Turkey on 29 October 1923 with Kemal as the new nation's first president. While this resolved the issue of what to do with the political entity known as the Ottoman Empire and its Sultan, it failed to come to grips with the religious issue of what to do about the Islamic caliphate, in which the Ottoman ruler filled a dual role as the secular leader, or Sultan, and Islam's religious leader, or caliph. The assembly had previously dissolved the Sultanate in November 1922 but had elected the ex-Sultan's cousin, Abdülmecit, as caliph. Although

Abdülmecit expressed support for the nationalists, he desired to retain as much prestige as possible, as well as the considerable subsidy he received from the government, and he had quite a number of supporters, none the least of which were the political opponents of Kemal. In addition to westernization and modernization, Kemal was an ardent advocate of secularism and despised the influence of religion in politics and personal lives. He threw himself into the process of ending the caliphate and began lobbying for change. In the end, it might have been Abdülmecit's repeated requests for money that tipped the balance in Kemal's favour. On 2 March 1924, Kemal pushed a group of bills through the new parliament. The first abolished the ministry of canon law thereby ending a law code based on religion; the second established a single system of public education thereby putting an end to religious schools; the third abolished the caliphate entirely. Though strongly resisted by Islamic clerics, some of whom occupied seats in parliament, the bills passed easily and were a significant political accomplishment for Kemal. The ex-caliph himself left Istanbul for Switzerland two days later. Most of the royal family followed, thus ending the 500-year reign of the Osmanli dynasty. Kemal was not quite finished with Islam, however, and parliament soon passed more laws disestablishing religious courts, lifting the ban on alcohol and easing laws on divorce and inheritance. Islam remained the official state religion but was effectively removed from official and daily life.

In 1924 Kemal, more or less by himself, wrote the new Republic's constitution. The new governmental architecture blended the powers of an American-style presidency with a European parliamentary system. The constitution expanded citizenship to Armenians, Kurds and Jews, giving them the right to vote and serve in the army. Great tensions continued to build up as Kemal consolidated his personal authority over the new government. He saw a number of prominent nationalists as competitors and systematically excluded them from the levers of power in Ankara. Chief among them were the war hero of the east Kâzım (Karabekir), naval hero Rauf (Orbay), army commanders Ali Fuat (Cebesoy) and Refet (Bele), and assistant speaker of parliament Dr Adnan (Adıvar). These men and others wound up in opposition to Kemal's People's Party and most were demonized and exiled from Turkey.

Problems erupted in the south-east with the restive Kurds, who still hungered for the independence promised them by the Allies at Sèvres in 1920. A Kurdish rebellion under Sheik Sait broke out in February 1925. Kemal turned to his trusted friend İsmet and sent him

Kemal at Yeşilkoy Airport (Istanbul) inspecting an American-made Martin B-10 bomber. Kemal was an ardent enthusiast and supporter of both military and commercial aviation. He also encouraged the sport of gliding and ensured that women were also allowed to become pilots in the Turkish Republic. (Stuart Kline)

Atatürk attending army maneuvres in the late 1930s. Until the end of his life Kemal retained an active interest in the army and in military affairs. (Mesut Uyar)

and the army to quell the rebellion, which was centred on the town of Diyarbakır, pitting 25,000 soldiers against about 15,000 poorly armed Kurds. Pushing laws through parliament that essentially granted him the authority to impose martial law, Kemal proceeded to crush the rebellion ruthlessly. The sheik and 46 of his supporters were defeated, caught and hanged for their treason. Thereafter Kemal implemented a 'policy of denial' (which lasted until 2009) in which the Kurdish identity, language and culture were forbidden in Turkey.

Ever the westernizer, Kemal famously left Ankara on 23 August 1925 to tell the Turks that, henceforth, they would wear European-style hats rather than the traditional red Ottoman fez. This was the beginning of an expanding torrent of secularizing laws that transformed Turkey into an essentially European state. For women, Kemal discouraged the wearing of the veil, ended polygamy and made civil marriages compulsory. What began as a series of comprehensive political changes extended into societal changes that fundamentally altered the Turkish way of life. Taken together these laws and policies are known today as 'Kemalism'. Kemal encouraged the founding of the Turkish Historical Society in 1930 to show the Turks what they had done in the past, and two years later established a Turkish Language Society. The most well-known impact of this was the introduction of a Latin alphabet to replace the Arabic-based Ottoman script. Kemal's quest to establish a Turkish identity went off course, however, when he advanced his 'Sun language' theory, which postulated that Turkish was the original core world language. In 1926, statues and portraits of Kemal began to appear in ever-increasing numbers, flouting the Islamic practice of the public representation of human beings. A year later, it was illegal to engrave religious phrases on public buildings. The European calendar was introduced and the day of rest changed from Friday to Sunday.

On 1 November 1928, at Kemal's instigation the parliament required all Turks to learn and use the new Latin-based alphabet. While this made integration with Europe easier, within a generation, this law cut the Turks off from their own written history. In 1931, Kemal introduced the metric system into Turkey replacing the complicated Ottoman system of weights and measurements. On 21 June 1934, the parliament passed a law requiring that all Turks adopt a family name. Parliament passed a law giving him the surname Atatürk or 'Father of the Turks.' At the same time, Ottoman titles such as Pasha and Bey were abolished. Kemal also gave women the right to vote in 1934. The educational curriculum was entirely secularized and a focus on the Turkish national identity came to dominate schools and universities.

In domestic policy, Atatürk encouraged agricultural self-sufficiency and created an industrial policy something like the Soviet five-year plans, which established factory production in Turkey. As a result, coal production skyrocketed, as did iron production, and the Turkish textile industry came into being as well. Internationally, he reached agreements with Britain and France regarding Mosul and Hatay provinces as well as successfully negotiating the 1936 Montreux Convention establishing a regime for the maritime transit of the Turkish straits. As Atatürk, he coined the phrase 'Peace at home, Peace abroad' which became Turkish foreign policy for the remainder of the 20th century.

Mustafa Kemal Atatürk. As president of the Republic, Atatürk rarely wore a military uniform often appearing in formal attire or in a coat and tie. To the end of his life he was committed to modernization and westernization and strove to display this in his personal life and habits. (Mesut Uyar)

A LIFE IN WORDS

With the exception of a brief memoir of his experiences at Gallipoli in 1915, Mustafa Kemal Atatürk never wrote an autobiography nor did he write books for public consumption. The sum of his writing was exclusively professional and dealt with very narrow military subjects. After he became president of the Turkish Republic he made a number of memorable speeches that were transcribed and widely published in Turkey, as were some of his letters and telegrams. Unfortunately for the English-language reader, none of these works have been translated into English and remain difficult to access in the west.

As a part of their responsibilities, Ottoman general staff officers translated foreign military manuals and books for use by the army. Kemal was fluent in German and also did this necessary function. In Salonika in 1908, Kemal translated and distributed Karl Litzmann's *Instructions for the Conduct of Platoon Combat (Takımın Muharebe*

Anıtkabir – literally 'Memorial Tomb'. Atatürk's mausoleum in Ankara is starkly modernist shrine to the enduring memory of the 'father of modern Turkey'. (Atatürk and Independence War Museum)

Talimi). He followed this in 1909 by translating a book on military ceremonies and then, in 1911, another on expeditionary force training. In 1912, he had time to translate and distribute Litzmann's *Instructions for the Conduct of Company Combat* (*Bölügün Muharebe Talimi*).

After the Balkan Wars, Kemal's friend Mehmet Nuri (Conker) gave a staff lecture at a training conference titled 'Officer and Commander' (*Zabit ve Kumandan*), which addressed army problems stemming from the defeat. Kemal could not resist commenting on his friend's thoughts and, while in Sofia on attaché duty, published a public response to Nuri's ideas in May 1914 titled *Officer and Commander; A Friend's Thoughts* (*Zabit ve Kumandan ile Hasbihal*). In this book, Kemal identified systemic failures of the Ottoman army in the war and was very critical of its leadership. He also took on the miserable performance of some of the officer corps in the execution of tactical operations and attributed it to the ignorance of doctrines. The book was typical of Kemal's lifelong tendency to take on the establishment. After Gallipoli, Kemal narrated a brief *Gallipoli Memoirs* (*Çanakkale'yi Anlatıyor*), which was largely anecdotal and personal. Later in September 1917, he wrote his unsolicited, inflammatory and highly critical report on the strategic direction of the war and sent it off to Enver Pasha. An English-language translation of this report may be found in the British official history of the war in F. J. Moberly's *The Campaign in Mesopotamia 1914–1918*.

As president of Turkey, Mustafa Kemal's most famous speech was a 36-hour weirdly personal diatribe that took six days for him to read. Delivered to the Grand National Assembly from 15 to 20 October 1927, the speech covered the events from the start of Kemal's personal involvement in the Turkish War of Independence (19 May 1919) to the founding of the Turkish Republic in 1923. About two thirds of what the Turks call 'The

Speech' (*Nutuk*) contain virulent attacks on his political enemies and competitors, including Karabekir, Rauf, Mersinli Cemal, Nurettin, Cafer Tayyar, Ali İhsan and a number of others. It is considered an apologia and a polemic and ends with an appeal to the youth of Turkey to defend the constitution and the nation.

The English-language reader must turn to the secondary literature to gain a more complete understanding of this man. By far the finest book available is Andrew Mango's magisterial 1999 study *Atatürk, The Biography of the Founder of Modern Turkey*, which is based almost entirely on Turkish sources and is exhaustively researched. Mango captures the detail necessary to understand the political and personal complexities that drove Mustafa Kemal to ever-increasing positions of responsibilities. A more recent, but brief, study of Kemal as a military commander is Austin Bay's 2011 *Ataturk, Lessons in Leadership from the Greatest General of the Ottoman Empire*. Bay's book summarizes the character of the man himself. Two of the most well-known books remain the very dated (1933) but splendidly titled *Grey Wolf: Mustafa Kemal, An Intimate Study of a Dictator* by H. C. Armstrong and the 1992 biography by Patrick Kinross, *Atatürk: A Biography of Mustafa Kemal, Father of Modern Turkey*. Important supplementary information about Mustafa Kemal's life and achievements may also be found in the works of the current author, as well as George Gawrych, Mesut Uyar, and Erik Zurcher.

The life of Mustafa Kemal Atatürk remains the subject of much study in contemporary Turkey. In Ankara the Atatürk Research Centre (*Atatürk Arastırma Merkezi*) supports a wide range of academic research and scholarly publications. Likewise, the Turkish General Staff's military history division also publishes extensively regarding Atatürk's military career and life and there are a large number of popular biographies in print as well.

Finally, the personality cult status surrounding Atatürk is ending in Turkey. It is impossible to read a Turkish newspaper today without coming across something about Atatürk and the current political scene. This is because Atatürk's vision for what he thought ought to be the driving forces in Turkey's political future (often called 'Kemalism' or the 'Six Arrows') – republicanism, populism, statism, secularism, revolutionism and nationalism are under daily attack in contemporary Turkey. The current ruling party, the Justice and Development Party (AKP), led by Prime Minister Tayyip Erdogan, is mildly Islamist and seeks to return the nation to more traditional ways. The AKP has desecularized public education and lifted the ban on women's headscarves in official locations. The party has imposed restrictions on freedom of the press and has successfully taken away much of the political power previously held by the military. That said, it is unlikely that the AKP will move the Turkish Republic too far afield from Atatürk's principles and it is probable that Mustafa Kemal Atatürk's enduring legacy will remain a parliamentary, secular and representative Turkish democracy.

BIBLIOGRAPHY

Bay, Austin, *Ataturk, Lessons in Leadership from the Greatest General of the Ottoman Empire*, New York: Palgrave Macmillan, 2011

Bean, C. E. W., *Official History of Australia in the War of 1914–1918: The Story of ANZAC, vol. 1–2*, Queensland: University of Queensland Press, 1981 (reprint of 1942 edition)

Erickson, Edward J., *Gallipoli, The Ottoman Campaign*, Barnsley, UK: Pen & Sword, 2010

Erickson, Edward J., *Ordered To Die, A History of the Ottoman Army in the First World War*, Westport, Connecticut: Greenwood Press, 2000

Hickey, Michael, *Gallipoli*, London: John Murray, 1995

James, Robert Rhodes, *Gallipoli*, New York: Macmillan, 1965

Lee, John, *A Soldier's Life, General Sir Ian Hamilton 1853–1947*, London: Macmillan, 2000

Mango, Andrew, *Atatürk, The Biography of the Founder of Modern Turkey*, Woodstock, New York: Overlook Press, 1999

Oral, Haluk, *Gallipoli 1915: Through Turkish Eyes*, translated by Amy Spangler. Istanbul: Türkiye İ Bankası Kültür Yayınları, 2007

Prior, Robin, *Gallipoli, The End of the Myth*, New Haven: Yale University Press, 2009

Sanders, Liman von, *Five Years in Turkey*, London: Bailliere, Tindall & Cox, 1928

Shaw, Stanford J., and Ezel Kural Shaw, *History of the Ottoman Empire, Volume 2: Reform, Revolution, and Republic: The Rise of Modern Turkey, 1808–1975*, Cambridge: Cambridge University Press, 1977

Smith, Michael Llewellyn, *Ionian Vision, Greece in Asia Minor 1919–1922*, New York: St. Martin's Press, 1973

Uyar, Mesut, and Edward J. Erickson, *A Military History of the Ottomans, from Osman to Atatürk*, Santa Barbara, CA: Praeger Publishing, 2009

Wavell, Archibald, *Allenby, A Study in Greatness*, New York, Oxford University Press, 1941

INDEX

References to illustrations and plates are shown in **bold**. Caption to plates are shown in brackets.